River Rat

By

Michael E. Oppitz

Published in the United States of America

ISBN 978-1-955243-99-5 (SC)
ISBN 978-1-956741-00-1 (Ebook)

Oppitz Publishing
220 W Expressway 83 Room 214
Mcallen, TX 78501 USAs
www.riverratmichaeloppitz.com

Order Information and Rights Permission:

Quantity sales. Special discounts might be available on quantity purchases by corporations, associations, and others. For details, contact the publisher at the address above.

For Book Rights Adaptation and other Rights Permission. Call us at toll-free 1-888-945-8513 or send us an email at admin@stellarliterary.com.

CONTENTS

PREFACE

W hile living in Houston, Texas, Michael Oppitz drove the staggering fourteen-hour distance, nonstop, on multiple occasions from Houston to Big Bend National Park where the Rio Grande is located. Lajitas in where he began most of his trips. There are many different options available to float the river in canoe or kayak The Colorado trip begins in Redford, just north of Lajitas. Most of his trips were through the upper canyons, which consisted of the Colorado, Santa Elena, Mariscal, and Boquillas. The lower canyons consist of many class II to IV rapids located closely together and are for experienced canoeists and kayakers only. Elevated river levels can easily change the class of a rapid Michael Oppitz floated the upper canyons in four to five days. The lower canyons took him five to eight days.

The Colorado Canyon contains the most rapids of the upper canyons, and they are all small and very enjoyable. It is a good opportunity to become accustomed using different strokes and finding out how the canoe/kayak responds. The next canyon is Santa Elena, and some whitewater experience is a requirement. That's why it is best to float the Colorado first.

The rapids of Santa Elena are Matadero, False Sentinel, San Carlos, Entrance, and Rock Slide. Even though the first four require some skill, Rock Slide can be challenging is elevated water levels. Floating through Fern Canyon and past Smuggler's Cave, the river access is 2.5 miles downstream.

The Mariscal Canyon begins at Talley where the Talley Ranch Road dead-ends at the river. This canyon contains many challenging rapids, but they are not dangerous. Still, it does require planning in advance, and some lining or portaging of canoes may be necessary. The 1,800-foot-tall canyon walls make for spectacular viewing. The rapids are eleven miles long, which end at the takeout at Solis. After that, it's another twenty miles through San Vicente and Hot Springs Canyons before entering Boqillas Canyon.

The lower canyons can extend from five days to ten days depending how long it takes to canoe 83 or 134 miles. Heath Canyon, just downstream from La Linda, is the put-in location, and Dryden Crossing is the takeout point. Some of the canyons with walls towering over two thousand feet include Heath, Temple, Maravillas, Big, Rocendo, San Francisco, and many others that offer gorgeous viewing and constant rapids to run. It is important to pack plenty of water and provisions, and purchase a permit to run these canyons.

INTRODUCTION

Big Bend National Park in southwest Texas is as rugged and majestic as it is beautiful. It is also a birder's paradise in spring, when over four hundred species of birds can be found in one location, especially for those who are serious about completing a big year. The Rio Grande that flows through its boundaries and also divides the border between Mexico and the United States is a dangerous river that is popular with canoeists and kayakers.

Robbie Jasper is a graduating high school student who lives in a family whose parents are controlling as well as neglectful toward his interests and needs. Mr. Jasper is an architectural engineer who is gone a lot and travels the world maintaining his family's wealthy lifestyle while Mrs. Jasper is more concerned about what others think about her than she does about her family.

Robbie's father schedules a ten-day canoe trip down the Rio Grande in an attempt to mend family bonds that have been taken for granted for years. Their trip is met with disaster with Robbie being the only survivor. Robbie embraces the grounded values, principles, and simple lifestyle of a river rat who finds and saves his life on the Rio Grande and becomes a river rat, himself. With Robbie's genius aptitude still intact, he is able to help his customers in ways that no one could have possibly foreseen.

CHAPTER ONE

"**M**r. Clemens, Mr. Waverley is here for your one thirty appointment." Mr. Clemens's secretary, Darlene, is a no-nonsense person whose PR and organizational skills rival the secretary whom she just recently replaced because she spent too much time gloating over her nail polish and shine and twirling her hair around her finger for hours. Darlene has well managed short brown hair, photo gray prescription glasses, and always dresses very smartly.

"Thank you, Darlene. Please show him in."

Mr. Waverley is an odd character and is someone who would stand out in a crowd. His reddish-brown curly hair nearly forms an afro, and his black rimmed glasses make him out to be a dork. Being of low stature, he has to walk quickly to keep up with most people who accompany him. His business-like navy blue pin stripped three piece suit saves him from others from staring at him too long.

Darlene ushers Mr. Waverley across a pristinely polished tiled floor toward a carefully crafted wooden door with chrome hinges and doorknob.

It's obvious this door was purchased with care and for a reason—to create a certain kind of intimidation for each individual who enters the office beyond it.

Mr Waverley carefully turns the chrome doorknob while the door opens without a sound. The several seconds it takes to peer around the door into a huge conference room with several people already sitting seems like several minutes. Intimidation immediately begins to take hold as Mr. Waverley enters.

The conference room is longer than it is wide in order to make room for a huge table. One side is completely constructed with eight-foot-tall windows that look out over the downtown area and the many skyscrapers. The parallel long sides of the room are filled with pictures of the projects that have been completed all over the world. They include bridges and buildings of all designs and construction materials complete shopping malls. The rear wall contains pictures of the administration personnel and department heads.

"Good afternoon, Mr. Waverley," Mr. Clemens says while grabbing his hand. "Welcome to Investment Solutions. Please have a seat and make yourself comfortable." As Mr. Waverley chooses one of the ergonomic chairs close to the head of the huge oval glass table, Mr. Clemens begins the introductions. "My name is Tyler Clemens, Vice President and head of Project Development. To your right is Connor Abernathy who is in charge of the Technology Department. Emily MacWilliam, to his right, is in charge of Research, and Preston Beauchamp is in charge of Communications. Please tell us what we can do for you," Tyler Clemens asks.

Michael E. Oppitz

Tyler Clemens is above average height with immaculately combed hair, and his three-piece striped suit fits him o a tee. His long legs accentuate his height to make him look taller than he really is. He speaks with a rich-sounding voice that immediately commands respect. Mr. Clemens began his career at Investment Solutions as an Intern straight out of college at Kansas State University. As a naive greenhorn in the world of business, he learned by mimicking others around him there was no substitute for hard work, and an 8 to 5 job never existed again if he were to succeed. It paid off in big dividends, and within fifteen years and some ass kissing, he was promoted to his current position. Connor Abernathy has short blond hair and a pale complexion. He complains that he burns too easily when getting out in the sun, so he always keeps a cap with him. He is a transplant from upper Michigan, so soaking up the sun and warmer temperatures is very new to him. His number two ranking in the IT department at the University of Michigan and a great placement program enabled him ground floor access where he could thrive in his environment and remain indoors. Emily MacWilliam is tall, good-looking, and her vibrant red hair extenuates all her natural features. Mr. Clemens began showing an interest in her ever since she scored second highest on the ACT test at her high school her senior year at Topeka High School in Topeka, Kansas. Her year-end essay was about the 110 year old history of her school and rich cultural heritage the school is known for. Upon graduating from University of Kansas in Lawrence, Kansas, with a degree in Business Management and Organizational Structure, Investment Solutions was a natural choice since she and Mr. Clemens kept in contact with one another during her entire college career. He also gave her an intern position as well. Preston Beauchamp is the nerd in the group. His thick black-rimmed

3

glasses give him away instantly. His intelligence and quick wit makes him a valuable member of the team. Preston grew up being bullied because he was so different, but smart. It wasn't until his high school years that he learned to use his intelligence to his advantage to minimize being bullied when he was asked constantly to do homework for the assholes who tormented him during his younger hears.

"Well, Mr. Clemens, the situation we have here about completing a viable jet engine assembly that can be presented to NASA within the time constraints they have demanded is a lot more complicated than Mr. Danielson, my boss, has foreseen. They have decided to outsource the construction of this particular hush-hush jet engine project and its components to private contractors and determine if this process will be successful for future projects and also prove to be less costly. Because of the complicated disciplines involved in the construction of this particular jet engine and components, Mr. Danielson has identified at least three other companies that provide the expertise required for its construction. However, since you are making the final assembly and shipping the final product to him, he has delegated you to contact all companies involved to make this happen," Mr. Waverley says.

"I see," Tyler Clemens ponders. "Has Mr. Danielson done business with these companies before?"

"He has, and with much reservations," Mr. Waverley replies while slowly bowing his head in embarrassment.

"What do you mean 'with much reservations'?" Tyler Clemens asks. "The businesses are well established and have good reputations for the products they produce. It's just that Mr. Danielson does not like doing business with the individuals of those companies who make those types of decisions," Mr. Waverley says.

"Mr. Waverley," Tyler Clemens snaps back, "do you really think it is the fault of those individuals, or is it a personality conflict problem Mr. Danielson has created himself? Honestly, it sounds childish to me. Anyways, please explain to me the companies involved, their specialties, the contact individuals of those companies, and the processes your boss has identified."

"Very well," Mr. Waverley says. "The first company is called EnTech, which specializes in engine components and specs. The contact person is a very boisterous individual by the name of Clarence Patterson. He likes to boast about all his hunting and fishing trips he takes on company time with company funds. He and my boss don't get along at all because of conflicting personalities and also concerning company values and principles. Mr. Patterson has been complaining lately about whether to take another one of his expensive trips or paying for his daughter's summer ice skating lessons."

"The next company is called Computer Solutions, which specializes in computers for all types of aircrafts and guidance systems. They will be instrumental in designing the computers and relay components that will communicate with the new jet engine. The contact person is Marvin Tillman. Mr. Danielson has difficulties working with him because of his OCD and his unwillingness to bend rules and time constraints. He likes doing things his way, and his way only." "The last company is called Pruitt's Electrical, which specializes in all things electrical. Xavier Pruitt, the contact person and owner, prides himself on being a small business with big solutions for aeronautical problems. His business can design any type of electrical systems for the most sophisticated aircraft. He has contacts all over the world and likes to design and build related components that require his specialty electrical needs. Therefore, he and my boss butt heads a lot because he goes beyond the scope of electrical and wants to expand out too much."

Finally getting agitated, Preston Beauchamp whispers to Emily MacWilliam, "What a bozo this guy is."

"Bozo, bozo. Where have I heard that before?" Tyler Clemens says under his breath. "That kid. That kid on the Rio Grande. He called this guy a bozo and said he was the key. He was right, and he knew it before we did. He *is* right, and it *will* work. Now all I have to do is remember what he said—or at least, suggested—because it is going to work. It's going to work and right now."

Tyler Clemens bows his head for a moment as if in deep thought. With a sigh that could be heard all the way across the huge conference room, he slowly lifts his head, gazes at his fellow companions, then looks at Mr. Waverley and says, "Mr. Waverley, thank you for coming all this way and sharing all this information with us and being honest about your boss's inability to communicate with those individuals who make the important decisions. I don't appreciate, however, the fact that Mr. Danielson is delegating his authority for something he should be doing himself but yet takes credit for someone else's efforts, so this is how things are going to work."

"Your boss is taking responsibility for inspecting the completed assembly of this jet engine before being presented to NASA. However, he is being a coward by delegating the important and necessary processes of this project to someone else, me. This is what you are going to do without fail, otherwise, I will complete my own inspection of the completed jet engine assembly, take responsibility for it, and make my own arrangements to present it to NASA. If NASA wonders why changes have been made without their permission, that's something *you* will have to explain to your boss. If you are listening closely, this is the way it's going down," Tyler Clemens says demandingly.

"You have to tell your boss that he is not going to receive the completed jet engine assembly so he can present it to NASA because I am going to do it instead. If he wants to remain in charge of this contract with NASA, he needs to do the following: He must contact Clarence Patterson at EnTech and make the arrangements himself for the necessary components and specs that will be used for designing and assembling this new jet engine project. He is also going to offer to pay for his daughter's summer ice skating lessons to develop good will between the two and for future business relations. That way, he can take his expensive vacation. You are then going to tell your boss to have Mr. Patterson contact Marvin Tillman at Computer Solutions to design all the computer systems and components that will communicate with the jet engine according to his design specs. Your boss will call Mr. Tillman to confirm their conversation."

"The last call will be to Pruitt's Electrical to tell Xavier Pruitt to design and construct the specialty electrical systems according to Mr. Patterson's specs and the computer systems designed by Mr. Tillman. Mr. Danielson will communicate to Mr. Patterson that his design specs of the new jet engine will be sent to each other's company accompanied by noncompeting secrecy since this is a new jet engine design for NASA. Tell your boss that he needs to schedule ongoing conference calls with all the companies working on this project so they can communicate and work together," Tyler Clemens states in a demanding voice. "Also, Mr. Waverley, your boss will have no complaints with me, or I will take over this project after assembling all the jet engine components and doing the initial inspection myself, leaving him high and dry. Do you understand everything I have said, Mr. Waverley?"

Mr. Waverley looks at Tyler in a dumbstruck trance not knowing what just happened. His trance seems to be unprecedented and annoying until Mr. Beauchamp says, "Are you OK, Mr. Waverley? Is there anything I can get you?"

After what seems to be a minute or two, Mr. Waverley silently stutters, "I think I have everything I need. If I have any further questions, I can contact you." He stumbles to get up out of his chair, and as if being drunk, he slowly and clumsily makes his way toward the huge wooden door. Grabbing at the doorknob several times, he finally opens it and disappears.

"Tyler, dang, where did that come from?" Preston says in amazement. "That kid."

"What kid?" Connor asks.

"That kid on the Rio Grande. Remember? Our guide with the funny name. When we were camping next to the river one evening, he overheard our conversation about this meeting, but none of us knew if or when it would take place. He said this guy, Mr. Waverley, would be the key, and he's the one who called him a bozo," Tyler replies.

"He's just a kid. What does he know?" Emily asks.

"He knew enough to guide my thoughts throughout this meeting to our benefit as well as for everybody else's. I mean, with his influence, this has become a win-win situation for everyone. How he knew, I have no idea. But he knew. As clear as day, he knew, and he wasn't afraid to voice it," Tyler says. "I wonder what else he knows?"

CHAPTER TWO

When Robbie's alarm goes off at 6:30 am, an arm protrudes from beneath the covers and slowly reaches for the alarm clock. Fumbling about, the arm finally whacks the snooze button silencing the obnoxious noise. Moaning and groaning can be heard from beneath the covers as he groggily throws the covers off of him and ponders whether or not to get up. As he stands up and walks over to his dresser, he dresses himself in a short-sleeved pastel-blue shirt that is obviously one size too large and relaxed-fit cream-colored painter's pants. Descending the huge walnut staircase and sliding his hand along the smooth walnut railing kept dust free by his meticulous mother, he can hear his mother is already in the kitchen making breakfast, which consists of the usual— eggs over easy, hash brown potatoes lightly crisped, sausage links, and a large glass of OJ. It seems like the perfect breakfast for any red-blooded American teenager, but to Robbie, eating this multiple times each week loses its allure. He would be happy with a bowl of oatmeal, butter, and brown sugar, and maybe a banana for extra flavor. Another favorite of his is just a banana with peanut butter. He tries voicing his opinion many times, but it is to no avail. His complaints fall on deaf ears. He gets the same old response from his mother, "When you buy the groceries, you can eat whatever you want. As long as you live in this home, mister, you will eat what is best for you." To Robbie, it's just another way for his mother to exert her control over him.

"Robbie, why are you wearing those ragged, outdated clothes? You march right back upstairs and put on something more appropriate and better fitting. I will not have you going to school looking like you have parents who can't afford decent clothes for you to wear," Mrs. Jasper scolds. "As long as you live in Cocktail Cove, you will dress appropriately. Do you hear me, young man?"

The Jasper house is more than a house. It's a mansion like all of the other mansions in Cocktail Cove. The huge eggshell-white mansion with mauve trim sets off the road about one hundred yards with a beautifully veneered concrete driveway lined with light-gray stamped-concrete accent. The black wrought-iron gate is remotely controlled, and every one of the Jaspers' five cars has its own remote control. Stepping off the driveway leads to a sweeping array of three long steps that ascend to the front entrance and is greeted by a huge wooden door at least eight feet tall. The door must weigh about a ton because when it is opened, the door is four inches thick.

Cocktail Cove is the name of the cove on Geist Reservoir on the outskirts of Indianapolis, Indiana, where the wealthy live. Marcus Shrenker, the original founder of the area who was eccentric and loved to party, built the first mansion. Others followed, and in time, the party life took hold quickly. Every weekend, parties, nudity, and drinking become commonplace, and the police stake out the cove just to make sure things don't get out of hand. When the parties begin, boats would be tied up together, creating a huge raft consisting of dozens or even a hundred boats where one can walk from one end to the other without ever getting wet.

"Yes, Mother. I hear you. But why can't you let me dress in my own personal style on occasion? I mean, a lot of my friends wear clothes that personify their true moods of the day. Or better yet, the twisted sister twins wear whatever they want according to the weather. Now, that's real choice," Robbie exclaimed shouting to the wind. He knew his mother was not listening, but he gave it a chance just in case. "Mother, did you hear me?"

Mrs. Jasper is of average height with just the right length of straight brunette hair with round-rimmed glasses. Everything about her is considered average so as not to rock the boat when it comes to fashion, personal expectations, friends, hobbies, and being a mother of an only child. She is more concerned about what others think of her than she does about herself. But she is the master of her household, and everything has to be in its place. She even rules over Robbie according what she thinks others will think about her and her son.

"Yeah, I heard you, son. Now make sure you wear something stylish that fits well," she says without missing a beat. When Robbie descends the picturesque stairway wearing a sky-blue polo shirt and fitted khaki slacks, his mother is very pleased. "Now, don't you feel so much better wearing those clothes than those horrible loose fitting rags?"

"Yeah, I guess." After finishing breakfast—or rather, choking down breakfast—Robbie says, "Mother, I want to watch the track meet after school. Several of my best friends are participating, and I want to let them know I am cheering them on and giving them my support."

"You know very well that's not possible," Mrs. Jasper says. "If you want to get that scholarship to Kansas State, you can't relax on your studies one moment. Besides, you have a big test in computer science today, don't you?"

"I already studied for it last week. Besides, with my photographic memory, I still remember what I studied a week ago," Robbie pleads. "That's why I want to watch my friends at track after school. I can study my chemistry tonight in half the time as everyone else. How about it, Mother? Can't I stay and watch just for an hour after school?"

"No, sir, mister," Mrs. Jasper reprimands. "You get home right after school and begin your studies."

Robbie is a good-looking boy. Tall and with well maintained brown hair and green eyes that drive girls crazy. His six-foot-two well- built frame makes him the envy of the football and basketball coaches. He has natural athletic abilities and yearns for the chance to participate in sports and to also run off much of his energy and resentment from his controlling parents. To his credit, he bottles his emotions and resentment until he can move away to college and experience some sort of freedom and normal life.

After breakfast, Robbie's walk to school is a solemn walk. With just over a week left before graduation, the weather is sunny and pleasant. He notices everything around him. The warm morning wind blowing on his face and making his hair fall in his eyes. Cirrus clouds hanging out at sixty thousand feet above him, birds darting in and out of the trees, and mayflies filling the air and creating isolated clouds with their multitudes. He can't keep from thinking about all the things he wants to do during his last year in high school. Many of his friends went out for sports simply because they wanted to. They all supported one another. Robbie's favorite sports are tennis, volleyball, track, water polo, and water skiing (or at least, trick skiing), and debate, if debate were classified as a sport. He is good at everything in which he participates, but he is not permitted to participate as long as the scholarship to Kansas State hangs over his shoulders.

Even though Robbie is a certified genius, he doesn't feel like one because of his limited choices. He could have graduated from high school two years ahead of everyone else by quizzing out in a lot of his classes, but his parents wanted him to have the full high school experience, whatever he thought that meant to them. When he became bored with the classes that were available at high school, he began taking college classes to fill his academic needs.

His walk to school this morning seems like forever since his mind is swimming full of questions about why he can't do one thing for himself. With a limited amount of time left, all he wants to do is hang out with his friends and enjoy the simple things. With so much tension starting to build up in his mind, he begins shouting to the wind, "Why do I have such controlling parents? Why can't I do anything for myself? Why can't I enjoy myself these last weeks? Don't they know I'm getting close to burnout?"

His remaining walk to school is in a solemn slumber oblivious to everything around him. As these thoughts consume him, Christine tries

14

getting Robbie's attention. "Robbie, what's going on? *Robbie*, do you hear me? Robbie, aren't you listening?"

Christine is Robbie's best friend —they have gone to school together since kindergarten. She is relatively short compared to him, standing just a mere five feet three inches. Her natural hair color is strawberry blond, but she hides it with a light brown overtone with blond steaks. She always appears upbeat, which is somewhat of an annoyance to Robbie. Still, her persistent nature when she is around him keeps him grounded with his feelings and on track with what his parents want from him.

"Oh hi, Christine. I'm sorry. I have so many things going through my head right now. I didn't mean to ignore you. What's up?"

"What do you mean 'what's up'? What's wrong, Robbie? You seem more distant than I have ever seen you. I'm worried about you. Let me in," Christine says compassionately.

"For the first time, I feel more confused and angry for missing out on my high school experience. My parents' idea of a high school experience and mine are completely opposite. Besides getting A's in every class I have taken, I feel like I missed out on everything. I never get to do a single thing I want to do. So what if I will be considered as a Sophomore when I begin college at Kansas State. My high school experience will be gone, and I'll never know what I missed," Robbie shouts.

"Hey, don't shout at me. You're my best friend, Robbie. All you have to do is tell me what I can do, and I'll do it. That's what friends are for."

"I'm sorry, Christine. You *are* my best friend, and this is not the first time you have let me bend your ear. I'm just frustrated, and I don't know what you or I can do about it," Robbie says dejectedly.

"Well, I guess all you can do is keep trudging along, looking for the light at the end of the tunnel," Christine says, trying to patronize him.

As they walk through the main doors toward the commons area, Christine asks, "So, Robbie, what finals do you have coming up next week?

"Since I handed in all my assignments in physics a couple weeks ahead of schedule, my teacher said I don't have to take the final. Mr. Otto, in calculus, said I can opt out of his final if I help him with a visual exercise in advanced linear equations," Robbie says, nonchalant.

"I still can't believe Principal Malloy let you take both of those classes in one semester. Who, in their right mind, would put themselves through that kind of punishment?"

"Actually, Christine, it's no big deal. I just told Principal Malloy that if I can't go out for sports, I might as well expand my brain. At least that's one muscle that would be getting exercise," Robbie tries to say jokingly.

"Right. That's very funny coming from you. Since you don't want to attend any of the local universities that the great state of Indiana has to offer, what else do you want to become besides a vet at Kansas State."

"Kansas State has one of the best veterinarian schools in the entire nation. They fill their quota of students with resident students before considering out of state applicants. Therefore, getting in is just the beginning. I was told by the student counselor that many students move to Manhattan, which is where Kansas State is located, find a way to establish residency before enrolling as a resident. This all hangs on the hopes that they will be accepted into vet school when they do apply. I was able to skip all that nonsense when the dean of the vet school was made aware of my parents' intention to make a sizable donation if I am able to apply right away. Instead of allowing me to make it on my own in college, their long arms of control are following me the whole way.

"Besides completing vet school, I also want to get a double degree in nuclear engineering, then transfer to their Salina campus and get my aeronautical engineer degree. Who knows what I can do after that?" Robbie finally says with enthusiastically.

"Unbelievable," Christine says with amazement. "Is that all If I had your genius aptitude, I'd be dizzy as hell right now. By the way, what plans do you have for the summer? Will I see you?"

"My parents told me last week that they have something special planned for me to celebrate my graduation. I have no idea what they have planned or whether or not I will like it. I'll let you know as soon as I can so we can plan some time together."

"You'd better," Christine says scornfully. "Hey, what about the cove this weekend? Are your parents planning on taking out their boat?"

"I will ask, but I hope so. While they are yakking with their friends, maybe we can get together with everyone else— or better yet, just ourselves," Robbie says hopefully.

"Yeah, just let me know. I hope we can at least do something together."

CHAPTER THREE

Robbie walks home after his day at school after acing his computer science test and helping others in both physics classes. What he considers nonchalant would be a class schedule nightmare to anyone else. To him, it's just another day at school, especially since he can't participate in sports.

Instead of announcing himself by fishing for the iron gate remote in his pocket and walking the hundred yards up the driveway to his house, he jumps over the iron fence obscured by overhanging maple branches and leisurely walks the remaining distance through the pristinely maintained grass and landscaping. Just once he would like to see a weed or a flower out of place so he could know what it would be like to feel normal.

Robbie opens the garage door and walks past the five cars perfectly parked the same distance from one another. Entering the kitchen area from the garage, his mother greets him by saying, "Hi, Robbie, how was school?" He knows she's not really fishing for an answer but rather just making chit chat.

"Same as usual. Aced my computer science test and not much left to do in physics classes," Robbie says calmly. "Hey, by the way, are you and Father planning on taking out the boat to the cove this weekend?"

"Yes, we talked about it. Any certain reason why?" she asks uncertainly.

"Some of my friends are going to be there, and I would like to hang out with them, that's all."

"OK, that sounds fine. Your father and I will let you know. When your father gets home, we want to talk to you about your graduation present."

"When will he get home?" Robbie asks.

"He is finishing up with the Indonesian project, and his plane arrives at the airport tomorrow afternoon. He should be here for supper. We can talk after that," Mrs. Jasper replies.

Robbie gets his height from his father, and Mr. Jasper is an architectural engineer who works for an international company designing and building structures all over the world. He has dark-brown hair, almost black, with dark eyebrows and a dark mustache. He has wanted to grow a handlebar mustache since his college days, but his image and line of work has not allowed him to do so. He is a gentle-natured man with a firm voice but soft eyes. He finds it difficult to express his love for his son mostly because he is not home much. He talks about Robbie's studies and studying for his scholarship but doesn't ask about his friends. He always says he is doing it for his family.

The next day results in another day at school as usual. Robbie's classes remain uneventful. Christine catches him during lunch in the commons area and asks, "Hey, how's it going? Anything worth talking about, being Friday and all?" She dresses very casual on Fridays, and the tight-fitting jeans show off her curves more than usual. The flower print of her shirt matches her exuberant personality.

"No, dull as usual. With classes winding down before finals, I find my teachers reaching for things to do just to keep everyone busy. Can't wait for summer to get here."

"You and I both," Christine says. "Let me know when you decide about tomorrow so we can plan our get-together at the cove."

"Will do. What classes do you have left today?" Robbie says inquisitively.

"All I have left is advance chemistry and history. Nothing to write home about."

"Well, take care, and I'll get back with you," Robbie says as he gets up and walks away to his next class.

CHAPTER FOUR

R obbie and his mother wait at the airport for Mr. Jasper to walk out through the main doors. Robbie has been to the airport many times, dropping off his father since he travels a lot with his work.

He knows the airport by heart, and his father knows exactly where he will be to pick him up each time he arrives briefly before having to leave again.

"Mother, what time did you say Father's plane arrives?" Robbie asks. "About four thirty pm, and I texted him to look for us just outsid the main doors."

"Oh, there he is. Right over there. Good, he sees us." Robbie can hardly hold in his excitement.

Robbie is nearly a spitting image of his father except that Mr. Jasper is more handsome. He's all business when it comes to his work, and sometimes it takes a little while for him to relax and become a father. The shorter time he has at home before taking off again for work, the less Robbie sees a father image in him. But when Mr. Jasper can stay home for more than a few days, Robbie gets his father back.

Robbie jumps out of the car, not seeing the scornful look on his mother's face, and runs toward his father. He embraces his father even before he can put down his briefcase and luggage. "Father, I'm so glad your home. Can't wait to spend some time together."

"Me too, son. I hope to be home for more than a few days this time, so I'm looking forward to it as well. Let's go get your mom and go home."

The airport is on the southwest side of town, so the drive home is about thirty minutes, depending on the traffic. Driving up to their big wrought-iron gate, the remote works smoothly, and the hundred yards to the house takes no time at all. The lawn is pristinely manicured, and the bushes are kept trimmed so nothing looks out of place.

"It's great to be home again. Really missed seeing everything perfectly maintained," Mr. Jasper says. "I hope we can really spend some quality time together this time, Robbie. I won't let anything get in our way to having a great time together."

"Me too, Father. I'm really looking forward to it."

As the garage door opens, Mrs. Jasper parks the car just the right distance from the others. Entering the kitchen through the garage door, Mrs. Jasper begins making dinner while Robbie and his father relax in the family room.

"So, Father, tell me about your last trip to Indonesia. What were you working on?" Robbie asks. Robbie knows his father is all business when it comes to his work, so he was waiting for some dry explanation about what he does.

To his surprise, Mr. Jasper opens up to Robbie by saying, "I'll tell you, son, my work has become more demanding of my time and technical abilities to keep the company I work for more competitive and more desirable to our prospective customers. The more stress I have, the more I think about you and your mother. It seems like I want to be here with you more and more. I feel like I have missed out on your high school experience, and I'm truly sorry for that. I do what I do to keep you and your mother in this lifestyle, but it comes at a high price. I want to do whatever I can to help make up for that. In fact, your mother and I want to discuss with you a graduation present we want to share with you. Just the three of us. Does that sound like something you would be interested in?"

"Interested in? I can't wait. What is it?" Robbie says excitedly. "Well, your mother and I want to share it with you together. Perhaps we can discuss it during dinner. Honey, what time do we eat?"

"Right about now. I had everything prepared ahead of time knowing you would probably be hungry after a long plane ride. You two make your way to the table so I can bring in your dinner," Mrs. Jasper says.

Setting at their usual places at the dining table, Mrs. Jasper dishes up supper and sets it in front of them. Robbie says right away, "What would be the possibility of taking the boat out to the cove this weekend?"

Mrs. Jasper stops in her tracks for a few seconds giving Robbie her normal stare while Mr. Jasper is unaffected. Mr. Jasper replies, "I was hoping for a weekend just the three of us, but that sounds like a good idea, at least for a while."

"Honey, we can talk about that later. Isn't there something else you want us to talk about with your son?" Mrs. Jasper says.

"Yes, there is. Son, we want to talk about your graduation present, and this is not some materialistic gift that will catch dust after its use has lost its allure. The one thing we cannot replace is the time we have missed during your high school years. So we want to try to make up for some of that. We want just the three of us to spend some quality time together on a canoe trip down the Rio Grande River in Big Bend National Park in Texas. Have you heard about that before?" Mr. Jasper inquires.

"No, I haven't. Didn't even know it existed. How do we get there, and when do we leave?" Robbie asks excitedly.

"Well, if it's OK with you, we leave the evening right after your graduation," Mr. Jasper says.

"What do you mean if it's OK with me? That means I can't attend any graduation parties and see my friends before I leave. I guess that's one item you forgot about when planning my life for me. You know what, I don't care if you put the boat in at the cove this weekend. I'm going there anyways to see my friends. I'm sorry, but I've lost my appetite. Please excuse me. I have some phone calls to make to see my friends before I leave," Robbie says defiantly.

"You act as if you will never see them again. Now, mister, you get back here right this moment. Don't disrespect your mother for making this wonderful dinner for us," Mr. Jasper scolds Robbie.

"Very well. It's not the end of the world, but I would like to let you know that your planning leaves a lot to be desired, Father."

"Received," Mr. Jasper replies. "I sincerely apologize for not leaving you time for things that are important to you. I am sorry, son. I will do whatever I can to make up for some of my shortcomings. I hope that someday you will come to forgive me. I am trying, son, but as you can see, I still have a lot to learn. My time away from you and your mother has robbed me of the talents I need to make my family happy. I have forgotten how to be a father to you and a husband to your mom. With the time off I have taken for these next few weeks, I hope to learn from you how I can be more of a father again and make some memories worth remembering. Don't hesitate to give me helpful hints when it's necessary."

"Thank you, Father. That does mean a lot to me. I do hope we can put the boat in this weekend, and I'm glad you will be with us for the next few weeks. There is so much to do and time to make up," Robbie says.

"Yes, you are right, son. I do have shortcomings when it comes to my own family. We will have a great time at the cove this weekend, and I hope you have a great time with your friends. I really am looking forward to our time together on the Rio Grande. I hope it will be a great bonding time for us. Please give me a chance, son. It means so much to me."

"I look forward to it, Father."

CHAPTER FIVE

Spending time in Cocktail Cove was as rewarding as ever, with perfectly clear blue skies and no wind. A record number of boats showed up to create one of the biggest floating rafts in a long time, about a hundred boats in all. Even though it was late May and the water was still cold, that did not keep people from cooling off with a quick swim when the temperatures spiked over ninety degrees. Robbie's parents were off somewhere, twenty some boats away, yakking with their friends and drinking wine and beer while Robbie was with his friends—drinking soda, of course (with an occasional rum spike).

The cove is protected from the constant winds that can blow across the reservoir with its tall cliffs. The water clarity is quite good on most occasions, so seeing underwater allows divers and fisherman to sight see fish during early mornings and at sunset. Shrubs have taken hold in the rocky crevices, and small trees grow on the outcroppings. Birds fly in and out of the holes that have been made in the soft limestone.

Robbie's friends were all together, taking up two whole boats. "Hey, Christine. Your swimsuit really does your figure justice. Didn't know you had such shapely curves since they have been hidden under those loose- fitting clothes you like to wear all the time."

"You're not so bad yourself, Robbie. You should give you and your physique more credit," Christine says with a big smile. "It's great to see all our friends in one place for a change."

"That's an *amen* from me since I'm not permitted to attend any sporting events where my friends usually gather without me. I'm hoping this will happen more often throughout the summer."

"So, Robbie, what kind of plans do you have for the summer?" Susan shouts over the noise of all the conversations.

"After graduation next weekend, my parents are taking me on a canoe trip down the Rio Grande River in Texas. It's supposed to be some kind of bonding trip so we can get closer as a family. Can't say it will work, but it seems worth a try. At least, it's important to my father," Robbie says. Billy chokes on his drink while trying to interject, "A canoe trip. Down the Rio Grande. Have you or anyone in your family been on a canoe trip before?"

"Well, actually, no. The only time I've been on the water is in our speedboat. The guides will tell us what to do and how to do it, I suppose."

"You're guessing, Robbie," Susan shouts again, being the farthest away in the two boats. "If you make a mistake, it could be hazardous to your health."

"While all this concern over me? I can take care of myself," Robbie scolds.

"Never mind, then. We're just concerned for you since we don't get to see you that much. You *will* watch out for yourself. I mean, we do want to see you again," Susan says.

"Yes, of course. I want to come back in one piece."

"When do you leave?" Sebastian asks from the next boat. "Not to my liking, but we leave right after graduation.

It really pisses me off that my high school experience will culminate without being able to attend any rite-of-passage parties. I never get to make a fool out of myself, and I was really looking forward to it," Robbie complains.

"Hey, everyone, we need to have our own rite-of-passage party for Robbie when he gets back in one piece," Christine says jokingly.

A few people speak up at once, talking for everyone else, but Robbie knows that it probably won't happen. It's a nice gesture just the same.

After graduation is over and all family and group pictures have been taken, Christine tracks down Robbie, runs up to him, grabs a hold of him and plants a huge kiss on him. "I don't know what got into me, but I just had to show you how much I care about you, Robbie. You'd better come back in one piece, or I'll come find you."

Robbie has never seen Christine this affectionate toward him before. He thought they were just best friends. "I had no idea, Christine. If I don't come back, I'll be looking for you." "Don't joke around with me. I'm serious now. You are important. I want you to know that. I'm hoping you will want to spend more time together when you return."

"I would love that. I want you to know that, and I'm serious," Robbie says.

"Good. It's settled, then. We'll be thinking about each other, and you come back in one piece," Christine finally responds with a big smile on her face.

They hug each other tightly in an embrace that must have lasted more than a minute, then Robbie kisses her. "I was hoping you would do that," Christine says affectionately. "I look forward to more of that."

"Me too. Take care," Robbie says, looking over his shoulder as he disappears around the corner.

CHAPTER SIX

L eaving for the airport right after graduation is difficult for Robbie. He yearns to be with his friends, especially Christine. His thoughts are flooded with new emotions he's never had before, and now they are centered toward Christine. As the airport shuttle leaves from his house, there is silence in the air. No one really knows what to say. Robbie's parents know now that they made a mistake by arranging the departure time right after his graduation. They suddenly realize that they robbed him of the most important time with his friends. This is Robbie's rite of passage, and probably one of the most important times in his young life. They can only sulk as they witness the defeated expression on his face. Mr. Jasper whispers to his wife, "What have we done?" Mrs. Jasper's blank expression says it all to her husband.

As their flight into Midland, Texas, begins to descend on the airplane's final approach, Robbie and his parents find a way to make ends meet. Robbie realizes that it is futile to fight the fact that he is now on vacation with his parents instead of being with his friends. He's no longer sulking in his own misery, but finds a way to become a part of the family again, enjoying being with his father. He is stuck now, and now it's time to make the most of it. Robbie and his parents finally start having harmless conversations with just thirty minutes left to their flight. It has only taken four hours for them to find a way to make this happen. Now everyone seems to be enjoying themselves being together and as a family.

"So, Father, where do we go from the airport?" Robbie asks harmlessly.

"Well, son, we find our rental car, then it's a three-hour drive or so to our destination, which is Lajitas, Texas. We continue on Highway 385 through half the park before heading west to Lajitas," Mr. Jasper says.

"What does southwest Texas look like?" Robbie replies with some excitement.

"I don't know, son. I guess we'll find that out together."

After their plane lands in Midland, Texas, and taxis to their gate, disembarking goes smoothly. They make their way to the car rental port in the airport and get directions to the park entrance of Big Bend National Park. Their destination of Lajitas is within the western edge of the park, right on the Rio Grande. It's a very popular place for launching canoes in order to float down the different canyons of the Rio Grande. The river is actually the border between the United States and Mexico. Some locations are watched closely to prevent illegal immigrants from crossing the river from Mexico into the United States.

Leaving the airport, they venture west on I-20 for a little way before finding Highway 385 south toward the park. Southwest Texas is mostly dry but very beautiful. Native scrub grass dots the landscape, accompanied by prickly pear cacti and other vertical cacti. There is nothing flat about southwest Texas. There are rocky outcroppings, bluffs, and depending on the time of year, flowers color the landscape everywhere. The rocky landscape was made possible through eons of wind and water erosion. The expanse is tremendous, and there is always something new hidden around every turn or at the beginning of each horizon.

Big Bend National Park received its formal name in 1944 as a bill presented to Congress by President FDR, which included eight hundred thousand acres. Unbeknown to most Americans, it was considered an international biosphere reserve in 1976. The native Indians who colonized the area said that after making of the Earth, the Great Spirit dumped all the remaining rocks in Big Bend. The Spanish explorers thought the land to be uninhabitable. The desert area of Big Bend is blocked by mountains on three sides, which prevents much rain to fall there. The Big Bend area is not without life. It contains 450 bird species, 75 mammal species, and 67 amphibian and reptile species. Birders from across North America converge in Big Bend in spring for one of the most glorious encounters of bird species found in one location at one time. Even though Big Bend is a desert and water levels drop considerably during summer months, being caught within the canyons during a downpour upstream outside of park boundaries can be very dangerous to anyone canoeing at the time.

Reaching the park entrance, the entire landscape changes even more to simply awesome. The park ranges in elevation from 1,800 feet at the Rio Grande to 8,000 feet in the Chisos Mountains. Big Bend National Park is rugged and beautiful at the same time. Rocky outcroppings turn into mountains. There's something new to see every half mile. At the park's

33

halfway mark is the visitor's center. There, turning west and following the road signs to Lajitas is easy to find. That's where the different tour groups and guide services are located.

"Well, everyone, we made it to the park just fine. I didn't hear much talking until we hit the park entrance. Were you two sleeping?" asks Mr. Jasper.

"How'd you guess?" Robbie replies, answering with a half- conscience voice.

"You'll never see anything like this anywhere in the world. This is really awesome. Even with all my travels, this is simply something spectacular. Don't you agree?" Mr. Jasper says fishing for a response.

"Totally awesome, Father. I agree this park is different from anything I have seen before. We're not in too much of a hurry to get there, are we?"

Robbie asks.

"You're right," Mrs. Jasper says. "Perhaps we can take our time to sightsee instead of hurrying along."

"All right, but I want to hear some interest in you two. Besides, I can only travel at forty-five mph at the most, so stay sharp," Mr. Jasper warns.

As they enter the city limits of Lajitas, Mr. Jasper says, "Hey, everyone, we're here. Help me find our outfitters."

"What's the name of it again?" asks Robbie. "It's called Southwest Texas Outfitters."

"Catchy, huh?" Robbie quickly replies. "Lajitas is more like the old West. This I can relate to since it mimics the Midwest a lot."

"According to the history of this area, the Spanish deemed this area uninhabitable, but some still settled here. If you look around, the Spanish architecture is very evident. Striking, huh?" Mr. Jasper says.

"Honey, is it true that Lajitas is mostly a tourist town, otherwise, what form of income is there?" Mrs. Jasper asks.

"Yes, sweetie. Floating the Rio Grande is the primary source of income, which also supports a resort and golf club. Must be nice, huh?" replies Mr. Jasper.

"If that's your thing," Mrs. Jasper quirks.

"I'm just ready to get in the river and maybe get wet. I've been in the car long enough," Robbie snapped back.

"There. Over there. There's our sign. Southwest Texas Outfitters," Mr. Jasper says.

"Good, let's get out and stretch our legs. Can't wait to walk around," Robbie says.

"If you want to get out and walk around, I'm going to find our guide and find out what time we leave," Mr. Jasper orders. Mr. Jasper gets out of the car with everyone else and walks toward the sign he saw from the road. "Hello, my name is Terrence Jasper. My wife, son, and I are scheduled for a ten- day float trip down the Rio Grande."

"Hello, sir, my name is Trevor, and I'm going to be your guide. Trevor is of slim build but muscular. His Australian bush hat and well trimmed beard and mustache fit the description of an outdoor adventurer very well. Living on the river and talking to so many tourists, he tries to maintain his original Outback accent as much as possible for their enjoyment even though he lost it a long time ago. He sports a sleeveless fishing vest instead of a t-shirt because it is cooler in the hot sun. His rich brown tan gets the attention of the young ladies, but he credits himself for not letting it go to his head. It looks like you are canoeing down the upper and lower canyons both. I'm glad to see you made good time from Midland. Most groups take their time sightseeing to find out that they just missed out on hours on the river. You and your family will get a lot of paddle time in today. Let's take care of some paperwork before we get started. Do you recognize these release forms I sent you via e-mail?"

"Yes, Trevor, there isn't anything here I haven't seen before. I can sign these so we can get underway," Mr. Jasper says. "Very good, sir. That should take care of things here,"

Trevor replies. "Let's go round up your family and luggage for a short shuttle up to Redford for the briefing so we can get underway."

Mr. Jasper yells to his wife and son who are wandering about, "Hey, you two, ready to get underway?"

"Are we! Let's get started. Can't wait to get on the river," Robbie says.

"Speak for yourself, Robbie. I would rather watch a movie of someone doing this than be in a hurry to do it myself," Mrs. Jasper quickly replies.

"Oh come on, Mother. How often will you ever have a chance to do something for the first time in your life like this?" Robbie tries to encourage her.

"I'm looking to you to keep me motivated and safe, Robbie. You will do that for me, won't you, son?"

"Yes, Mother. I will look after you the whole way. I promise nothing will happen to you except to have a great time," Robbie says loudly.

"OK. As long as you take care of me. I know I'll be safe. Thanks, sweetheart," Mrs. Jasper says affectionately.

CHAPTER SEVEN

G etting out at Redford, Mrs. Jasper takes hold of Robbie's hand and says softly, "Robbie, I know you must feel like we kidnapped you in order to spend this time together, but it's not like that at all. Your father and I wanted so much to be with you and to do something together that was totally different. We want this experience to last a lifetime and to be very memorable for you. Your father is so driven by timelines and deadlines, sometimes he doesn't know how to separate his work from his family until he finally has a chance to totally relax. And that doesn't happen very often. This is the first time I have seen him completely relax and show that he is really enjoying himself. I know you must have some animosity towards him for not being there for you or not responding the way you want him to, but I plead with you, son, to give him a chance, and maybe you'll see the side of him that you have always wanted to see."

"At first, I thought he was doing all this for him, which is why we left so suddenly after my graduation. It wasn't until we finally got to Midland that I realized that his intentions were real and that he showed some signs of caring. After all these years, I confess I really don't know him or his intentions, but I do understand now that this must be his way of showing it. With your blessing, Mother, I will give him the chance he desires and hope he comes through," Robbie says pleadingly. "Thank you, son. I don't want any friction between the two of you, and I know you will do your part to make this experience fun. I also realize he doesn't know how much of a genius you are and how incredible of a person you are for remaining humble about it. That shows incredible character, and I'm so proud of you," Mrs. Jasper says, giving Robbie a big hug.

As they all come together, Trevor asks them to bring their luggage from the shuttle down to the canoes. "If you all follow me down to the river, I would like to orient you with everything. I also want you to try on your life jackets I laid out for you to make sure they fit. You'll be wearing these the whole time we are on the river. As the canoes are being loaded with supplies, please open your luggage and place everything in these watertight bags I am giving you. Once they are filled, I will show you how to secure them so water does not dampen your belongings," Trevor says.

"How wet do think we will get?" asks Mrs. Jasper. "Since the water level can fluctuate during this time of year with rainstorms occurring upriver, the rapids we will be going over will fluctuate as well. These bags are just a precaution for when water splashes into the canoe where you will be sitting. It's nothing to worry about," Trevor says. "Now if you will kindly give me your attention, I would like to explain to you what kind of canoes you will be using."

"These are seventeen-foot ABS plastic Tejas canoes, the strongest made and are virtually indestructible. They have no keel on the bottom, so we can easily float over the slippery rocks of rapids. Even if the canoe becomes submerged, they will still float, even with you in it. So stay with your canoe at all times no matter what happens."

"What do you mean by 'no matter what happens'?" Mrs. Jasper quickly asks.

"Well, Mrs. Jasper, that just means that if a canoe would turn over for any reason, stay with your canoe because you will be floating a wild river," Trevor politely responds. "Please let me continue with the orientation. The sides are called the gun walls. The front is the bow, and the back is the stern. For the two who will be in the bow, this is how you enter and walk through the canoe safely. As you step in, grab hold of the gun walls with both hands. Walk through the canoe slowly while always keeping hold with your hands. Be sure you step in the middle at all times as not to rock the canoe. After a few attempts, you'll be pros at it."

"Who is the strongest paddler amongst you?" Trevor asks. "My son is," Mr. Jasper responds.

"OK. He will be in the stern of one canoe, and I'll be in the stern of the other. The stern paddler guides the canoe. Mr. and Mrs. Jasper, if you will take your place in the bow of your canoes, we can take our places and get underway. I want to show you all the forms of paddling once we are all situated and before we shove off," Trevor says.

Mr. Jasper helps his wife get in her seat, then he carefully walks through his canoe as instructed and has no problem. Robbie and Trevor shove off from shore just a few feet then get into their seats. "If you will please give me your attention, I want to show you how to use your oars," Trevor instructs them. He shows them how to grip their oars, the proper way to draw the oar through the water, how the stern paddler slows and guides the canoe, and how to scull through the water to keep control of the canoe in moving water. "When we get close to rapids, you will see a V shape being formed as the water flows towards the rocks of the rapids. That is called the notch. Finding that V and entering the rapids through it is called 'shooting the notch.' In order to float through the rapids slowly, you can back paddle, therefore maintaining control of your canoe and the speed. Always go through the notch, not around it. OK, as we shove off, stay close together at all times in order to keep communications easier."

As they slowly begin to paddle toward the middle of the river, Mrs. Jasper is first to speak up, "I have never been this close to the water in a boat before. It is quite unsettling. I'm not sure if I like this."

"Lots of people share your opinion, Mrs. Jasper, when it is their first time. Given time, it allows you to become one with the river and enjoy the solitude and peacefulness of the surroundings. Please concentrate on the beauty all around you, and it will be easier for you to enjoy your trip," Trevor explains.

"Please call me Eleanor, Trevor."

"Thank you, Eleanor. It makes it easier and more personal." "I think this is great," says Mr. Jasper. "I've never had this, uh, feeling of contentment before. I feel like I am under control, but yet, not. It is quite satisfying and very peaceful.

What about you, Robbie?"

Michael E. Oppitz

Robbie carefully places his hand in the calm water feeling the coolness and gentle massage affect as it trickles through his fingers and rushes over the hairs of his hand. The peacefulness that overtakes his senses rushes right to the very core of his being. With all the turmoil he has had to endure with his controlling parents, this new sense of feelings and emotions for such a simple thing as the cooling affect of this river blocks out everything around him. He seems to be in awe as to how the river has captured his being so easily. As he motions a figure eight in the water and splashes some of it on his face, he hears his father trying to say something to him.

"I think this is great. Never experienced anything like this before. I could really get used to this. I mean, on a steady basis even."

"You all keep talking. It's part of the experience," Trevor says. "Have any of you looked at a map of the Rio Grande River?"

"No, not really," Mr. Jasper replies. "I just left it up to you to inform us as to where we were going."

"Right. Well, the first canyon we will be entering is called Colorado Canyon. The water flows through it at a slow pace, so it will give you lots of practice getting in the groove with your paddling. Even though it has more rapids than any of the canyons we will float, they are small and very enjoyable. Take note of the different layers of volcanic rock on both sides," Trevor says. "The water erosion has exposed millions of years of rock giving way to different colors. This variation of rock is one of the main reasons the Rio Grande is so popular. As soon as we get to the tinaja, which is a natural spring rock pool, you can get out of your canoes, stretch your legs and go for a swim. That will occur about noon. We will also have lunch at that time as well."

42

After paddling for a while, Robbie hears something in front of him he's never heard before. "Trevor, what is that low roaring sound?"

"That roaring sound is the sound of the first rapids we are about to encounter, but no fret, it's just a small one like all of the ones we will encounter for the next two days."

"A small one," Eleanor shouts. "If that's a small one, what does a larger one sound like?"

"I don't want any of you to be alarmed. All of the rapids will announce their location to you by this roaring sound. The larger ones we will encounter, like in the Santa Elena Canyon ahead of us, will of course, be somewhat louder. By the time we reach those rapids, you will all be pros at this. So just relax and enjoy the rapids and have fun."

"Well, if you say so, Trevor. Robbie, I'm counting on you to keep me safe as we go through these rapids," Eleanor says in a worried tone.

"Mother, these first rapids that we are getting close to look like really small ones. I'm guiding our canoe, so listen to me as we go through, and I think it will be a lot of fun," Robbie tries to encourage her.

Hearing the roaring sound of the first set of rapids really awakes him to his surroundings. The water, still clear and soothing, has a different appearance to it. Instead of slow moving and tranquil, its pace begins to pick up, ripples start appearing, and more disturbances on the surface are evident all around him. The canyon walls on both sides of the river are tall according to what Robbie has seen before, and the different colors of clay and rock outcroppings capture his attention as if he were in a hypnotic trance. Even though Robbie needs to prepare himself mentally for the rapids just ahead, he can't get over how his senses have been captured by the magic of the river.

"OK, son, since we are almost there, can you see the notch?" Trevor says.

"Yeah, I see it!" Robbie shouts. "It's over toward the right side." "All right then. Robbie, guide your canoe over toward me, and stay behind me as we shoot this first notch. Should be a pushover. Just keep a steady hand on your oar and watch everything I do," Trevor says. Robbie swings his canoe behind Trevor, and both canoes float through the rapids easily and with no problems. "Wow, that was awesome!" Mr. Jasper exclaims. "I want to do more." "There will be plenty of rapids, Terrence, so you'll get your fix in no time. I'm glad you had fun with that. Eleanor, are you all right?"

"Yes, Trevor. I seem to be fine. Just a little unnerving, that's all. The water splashing up in my face was actually exhilarating, though."

"I'm glad you think so, and don't worry, Eleanor. You will get the hang of this in no time. I promise," Trevor tries to say reassuringly. Paddling comes so naturally to Robbie that he didn't have to think about what to do when positioning the canoe to go through the first set of rapids. As he continues to paddle in slow easy cadences keeping the canoe straight down the river, he finally has a chance to sense the gracefulness of the power of the river. The smallest correctness he exerts with his paddle changes the entire motion of the canoe. Robbie feels as if he is in complete control, but at the same time, not. The river is powerful, and he is still at the mercy of the current. Each stroke is a symbiotic relationship of how he can maneuver his canoe, and the current of the river allows it to happen. Robbie is quickly understanding how the solitude of his new surroundings has captivated his very sole, and he feels apart of the current, the warm sun beating down on him, the sound of the swallows dive bombing him in protest for invading their nesting sites, and the allure of the ever changing landscape.

As they continue downstream, Trevor points out on the left where some movie sets were filmed. "Just imagine, as you venture downstream and see the changing and exotic terrain, how some of the movies—*Dead Man's Walk, Streets of Laredo*, and *The Journeyman*—were filmed.

Each rapids they encounter have their own distinct roar. After a while, the roar of the rapids become commonplace. "OK, everybody, the tinaja is just up ahead. Follow me to the bank, and we'll get out for lunch. You can explore the area, relax, or take a swim while I get lunch ready," Trevor announces.

CHAPTER EIGHT

A s they beach the canoes, Robbie says, "I'm going for a swim." Robbie dresses down to his swim suit under his jeans and t-shirt. Jogging over to the tinaja in a spiteful cadence, little lizards make way as he trudges into their territory. He almost trips with a momentary lapse of attention while noticing a vulture soaring overhead. It didn't slow down his pace, though as he finally makes it to the swimming hole. Glancing down into the water, Robbie is amazed how clear the water is as he can see small fish swimming along the bottom nearly twenty feet down with such detail and clarity. As he jumps in, his words can easily be heard all the way back to the beach. "Wow, that water is cold!"

"What did you expect from natural spring water?" Trevor shouts jokingly.

"I don't know. This is all new to me. It stills feels good, though."

Trevor gets lunch ready with deli sandwiches and coleslaw. "Lunch is ready. Come on over."

As they sit around eating and enjoying the lunch Trevor assembled, Terrence asks the first question. "Trevor, how did you get into being a river guide?"

"I was an engineer for a huge company in Houston. About a year ago, I finally got fed up with the rat race and decided to come out here to work as a guide during the floating season. I had canoed these canyons many times before and just fell in love with its tranquility. During the winter months or until the following May, I work part-time for other engineering companies throughout Texas or hire on as a consultant. The relaxed lifestyle has saved my sanity, and I truly love it. Just wish I started this earlier."

"If you don't mind my asking, you look like you're in your late thirties?" Terrence asks.

"Actually, early thirties. The sun has aged my skin some, but I don't mind. If I die doing what I love, a little skin aging is no problem," Trevor replies.

"How many more rapids will we encounter before suppertime?" Eleanor asks.

"Are you thinking there might be too many for you, Eleanor?" Trevor replies.

"No, not at all. In fact, I think I'm getting quite used to them, so far. Just wondering how many more there are."

"Well, at our present pace, I think there are probably three or four more. But they are still small ones. Terrence, you'll have plenty of opportunities to get your fix," Trevor says.

"I can't wait. The more the merrier."

"Robbie, how about you? How are you holding up?" Mr. Jasper asks.

"I'm doing great, Father. Having the time of my life. Just taking it all in. I guess that's why I'm being kind of quiet. Just taking in the whole experience, but loving it. I could see myself doing something like this."

Mr. and Mrs. Jasper cringe at his remark, but to their credit, they don't say anything. Their hope is that their son attends Kansas State in the fall.

Lunch is delicious, and everyone gets their fill and more. "OK, everyone, back in your canoes. We have a number of rapids ahead of us before camping for the night. I have something special planned for dinner," Trevor announces.

The next few hours go by quickly. The amazing volcanic rock on both sides of the canyon are different after every mile. The peace and solitude to be had is mind-blowing. The rapids announce themselves with their own distinct roar, and going through them lends a sense of accomplishment and tremendous fun. Paddling is optional once the rapids are entered, except to maintain steering. It's just incredible and so peaceful.

"If you've had enough fun for a while, it's time to beach our canoes for dinner. With these tall canyons, darkness comes early. While you all stretch your legs and relax, I'll get a fire started for supper," Trevor says.

Robbie is the first one in the water, cooling off from the hot afternoon sun. His father joins him soon after. "Mother, come on in. The water's warm. You'll like it."

"Give me some time to think about it. I want to relax for a little while," Eleanor says.

"Eleanor, if you want to swim, now is the time to do it. Once the sun goes over these canyon walls, the temperature drops quickly. Do it now while you can," Trevor says.

"Very well, here I come."

Trevor starts the fire from the immense amount of driftwood available. He piles up a lot for the long darkness ahead when the sun sets below the canyon. "Supper's ready. The fire will dry you off quickly," Trevor announces.

As they settle in around the fire, Terrence asks, "So, Trevor, what's special about supper?"

"Being your first night camping on the Rio Grande River, I am cooking my special spiced potatoes in foil prepared in butter, sliced cheese, and summer sausage for munchies, and marinated chicken in my special sauce. Also, I brought five gallons of bottled wine so we won't run out. While the potatoes are cooking, help yourself to the munchies, and who wants wine?" Trevor asks.

"Eleanor and I are big wine drinkers, so we will put your five gallons to the test," Terrence speaks up. "Robbie, I also brought plenty of soda and bottled water. Help yourself."

"Robbie, I was told that this trip is your graduation present. Are you enjoying yourself?" Trevor asks.

"Immensely," Robbie replies. "I really am enjoying myself. This experience takes my mind away from all my other emotions and stresses from home and truly puts things into perspective for me."

"What kind of perspective, if you don't mind my asking," Trevor asks.

"When I attend Kansas State in the fall, I will be a sophomore working toward being accepted into vet school. They have one of the best in the entire country. I also want to get my nuclear engineer degree."

"Wow, that is quite the challenge, and I tell you engineering is no cake walk. But you seem to have everything lined out, and it looks like you'll do just fine. Good luck on your pursuits," Trevor says.

"Besides," Robbie adds. "If things don't work out, I can work as a guide, just like you. That has become my new passion."

"Now wait just one moment, young man," Eleanor scolds. "You are going to Kansas State, and that's final."

"Sure, Mother. Whatever you say."

Mrs. Jasper gives Robbie her dagger eyes, and nothing is said for the rest of dinner. Mr. Jasper, however, is not disturbed and continues drinking his wine and stuffing his face with munchies.

"What kind of sleeping arrangements are there, Trevor?" Eleanor asks.

"I'll show you how to set up your tents, or you can sleep under the stars. They are quite breathtaking. With the limited amount of viewing space there is because of the canyon walls, you might just get to see the Milky Way," Trevor responds.

After supper, darkness begins to fall fast. With the tents set up, Robbie elects to sleep under the stars in his sleeping bag. "Good night, sweetheart," Mrs. Jasper calls out to Robbie.

"Good night, Mother. See you in the morning."

Lying in the open air, Robbie intently takes in everything— the sounds of animals scattering the canyon walls, bird songs, the rustling of bats flying around in search of insects, and most importantly, the hypnotic sound of the water. The rush of tranquility swells all over him. He has never felt this perfectly relaxed, free from expectations, stress, and control from others. Here, he is alone with his own thoughts and emotions. As he lets the lullaby of the peacefulness guide his emotions, thoughts of Christine enter his mind. How he misses her. She would be the only one who would make this perfect. Except, things are close to perfect right now. He is truly enjoying this new and exciting experience completely. Sleep takes over as he ponders his newly found peace of mind.

CHAPTER NINE

Mr Jasper is awoken by the smell of freshly brewed open air coffee. "What an aroma. Excellent," he says as he emerges from his cocoon of a tent. "Best sleep I've had in a long time." "Bacon, eggs, biscuits, and gravy should wake up the rest," Trevor says hopefully.

Eleanor emerges shortly with her hair in a frizz. "I don't think anyone cares about what I look like out here. I'll fix it later, after breakfast."

"I don't think I would ever hear you say something like that at home. This is truly a new thing for you, isn't it, honey?" Mr. Jasper says with a smirk on his face.

"I think I would be in a frizz at home if my hair looked this. I think the outdoors is taking a hold of me as well. Can't explain it," Eleanor says.

"Robbie, honey. Breakfast is ready, son!" Mrs. Jasper yells. Robbie is already up and exploring. He pops over the hill with his Mother's announcement. "Best sleep I've had in a long time. Wonderful to be alive. The amount of reptiles and cacti around here are amazing."

"Come have breakfast before it's gone," Mrs. Jasper insists. "I had my fill already. It was wonderful."

"Trevor, I meant to ask you earlier but forgot for some reason. Is there any fishing to be had in the Rio Grande?" Robbie asks.

"Away from all the rapids, there is some fishing, but most people use this river for canoeing instead of fishing. In fact, that reminds me of a joke, if you are up to hearing it," Trevor says.

"Sure, Trevor. Have at it," Mr. Jasper says. "OK, here goes.

There were two fishermen on opposite sides of the river from each other. One fisherman was catching all the fish while the other one was catching none. At dusk, the luck of the first fisherman had not changed, not even a bite.

As darkness fell, the first fisherman yells across the river and says, "Hey, why are you catching all the fish while I haven't had a bite all day?"

"Why don't you come over here and I'll show you."

"How am I supposed to get across the river? I can't swim."

"Tell you what," says the other fisherman, "I'll shine my flashlight beam on the water, and you can walk over on the beam."

"Do you think I'm stupid or something? I'll get halfway across, and you'll shut off the flashlight."

"That sounds like a good parting joke to me," Mr. Jasper says. "When do you think we will be on our way, Trevor?"

"As soon as you all pack up everything in your waterproof bags and I get the tents rolled up, I'll put away the kitchen supplies. I imagine within half an hour," Trevor replies.

Once the canoes are loaded, Robbie and Trevor push off their canoes while Mr. and Mrs. Jasper begin paddling in the bows. "Soon, we will come to a couple of chutes that are popular and a lot of fun. At low water levels, you can probably go through them more than once. It's also a great spot to get out and swim. We will be out of the Colorado Canyon before the end of the day before entering the Santa Elena Canyon. I'll tell you all more about that later. For now, relax and enjoy the easy paddling until we make it to the chutes," Trevor says. They encounter several more small rapids, and Robbie says, "Hey, I think I finally got these rapids down pat. I want more, and I want bigger ones too."

"Don't worry, Robbie, once we get into Santa Elena Canyon, you'll have your hands full with more challenging rapids," Trevor replies.

"What do you mean more challenging ones, Trevor?" Mr. Jasper asks.

"The canyon walls are more narrow, taller. There's more rocks in the river, and the rapids are more challenging because the water is being squeezed as it goes through. It is a requirement to know how to paddle before entering Santa Elena, but you all have already met that. I think you will all be just fine," Trevor says. Trevor knows very well that he probably spoke too soon about whether or not his party really would be mentally tough enough to handle those rapids in Santa Elena, but he doesn't want them to worry about anything. Just to enjoy themselves. Whatever fate awaits them when they all get there, he must rely on his own leadership and experience to get them through unscathed. That is his hope, for now. A loud swallow goes unnoticed.

Robbie paddles with a big smile on his face, looking forward to getting there as soon as possible. He can't wait to test his newly found skill. Mr. Jasper is also smiling, but not as noticeably. When he looks back and sees Robbie, his face really lights up. Mrs. Jasper paddles slowly with a worried look on her face that does not diminish for quite a while.

After a number of hours and several more small rapids, they finally reach the chutes Trevor talked about. They look harmless enough, and it really is a popular place. The whole area is full of other canoeists playing, swimming, talking, and shooting the chutes. There is plenty of slack water before reaching the chutes, and they have to get in line in order to go through. There are probably ten to twelve other canoes waiting for turns in front of them.

"Mother, are you having fun?" Robbie asks.

"Yes, I am. It has taken me a long time to realize that I really needed this. And now I am enjoying myself," Mrs. Jasper replies. "How about you, son?"

"I am having a blast! Can't wait for bigger rapids." "Well, I'm enjoying myself with what we have gone through so far, and I hope it doesn't get any worse. I'm not sure I can take any more excitement than this," she says worriedly.

"Remember, Mother, I'll take care of you. I will keep you safe," Robbie exclaims.

"I know, son. It's my job to worry for both of us."

"Honey, Robbie seems to be very capable. Please trust him so you won't worry," Mr. Jasper pleads.

"Don't worry, I'll let Robbie do his job."

As they continue to drift, they get a little closer. With just a few canoes ahead of them, they can see how the others work the chutes. It appears they don't have to do anything at all. The water being squeezed through the chutes push the canoes along with quite some velocity. Since the chutes are so narrow, there's no room to paddle even if one wanted to. The others let the rush of water push the canoes through without any problems at all. When it's finally their turn, Trevor says, "Terrence, let's go through first and show the others how to do it."

"You got it. Here we go," Terrence says.

The velocity of water pushes them through in no time, and they didn't have to paddle at all. "Hey, you two. It's your turn. Don't worry, honey. There's nothing to it," Terrence says encouragingly.

As they enter the first chute, Mrs. Jasper starts screaming and yelling at the top of her lungs. In the fifteen seconds it takes to go through the first chute, she finally sighs in relief. Reflecting on how absurd she must have sounded, she starts laughing at herself. "What a little schoolgirl I must have sounded like. Please forgive me, everyone. Let's get to the next one, and I'll go first. That really is fun!" Mrs. Jasper shouts. As they continue on to the next chute, there are people everywhere lining the banks, swimming, relaxing in the water, and just having a great time. They are amazed how many people use this river, and especially this area. The current is slow, just like they have been used to, and there are other canoes in line for the next chute. They get in line while enjoying the peacefulness of the slow current. Robbie looks all around him, watching others line the banks cheering on the canoes going through the chutes. As their turn comes up, Mrs. Jasper elects to go first. She and Robbie enter the chute, oars out of the water, and the current of the chute pushes them along. Water splashes up into their faces, and Mrs.

Jasper sounds out with a gleeful yell of excitement. "Mother, you sound like you actually enjoyed that!"

Robbie shouts over the sound of the water.

"That was so much fun, I wouldn't mind doing that again.

What about it, son?"

"Sure thing," Robbie replies.

They turn around and watch Mr. Jasper and Trevor go through. "We're going through again!" Mrs. Jasper exclaims. "Who's with us?"

"Sounds great. We'll follow you!" Mr. Jasper shouts.

They get out of their canoes and pull them along the bank past the beginning of the chute, get back in their canoes, and paddle upstream to get in line again. This time, there are at least a dozen or more canoes already lined up. Waiting their turn, they go through again, and this time, they can hear people on shore yelling and shouting at them as they go through unscathed. "What a rush, Trevor!" Mrs. Jasper exclaims.

"I'm so glad you really enjoyed that, Eleanor," Trevor replies. "Let's beach our canoes and have lunch," Trevor says.

They disembark from their canoes with dozens of other people around them. Trevor unpacks the kitchen supplies and finds the container of deli sandwiches and leftover munchies from last night's supper. As they begin eating and everyone has smiles on their faces, Mr. Jasper says something completely out of context from his usual self.

"I can't remember the last time I have enjoyed myself so much being in such peaceful surroundings and sharing this with my family. I have missed out on so much, I can't begin to realize how much of life I have squandered away because of my selfishness. I hope you all can forgive me for not being there for you. I truly think this experience can be a turning point for me to be a better father and a better husband," Mr. Jasper pleads.

"That is probably the most beautiful thing you have said in a long time. I can't tell you how long I have waited for you to say something like that," Mrs. Jasper says. "Robbie, how about you?"

"I don't want this to end. I wish we can always think of us like this every day. I'm wondering if this how other families think of themselves, or if we are just now finding this out. If this does end when we get home, then I'll know it was just a dream," Robbie says sternly.

"I don't want it to be a dream, son. I will do whatever I can to make it real for you even after we get home. I want to be a part of your college experience, also, if you will let me." "I want you and Mother to both be a part of my life no matter where it takes me. I just need breathing room on my own at times, that's all," Robbie replies.

"Of course, son. We understand. At least now, I understand. Your happiness is extremely important. Our happiness as a family is extremely important," Mr. Jasper says.

"Honey, we both will do whatever it takes to be more like a family. The way I feel right now as a family, I want it to last as well," Mrs. Jasper says.

CHAPTER TEN

A s they finish lunch, Trevor interrupts, "When we get back into the canoes, we will be leaving Colorado Canyon and the lazy current conditions in an hour or two. Santa Elena Canyon is very different. The rapids are somewhat larger, but not dangerous. When we get to the first rapid, which is called Matadero Rapid—a class II rapid, or class III in higher water—I will go over our strategy. Right now, let's push off and enjoy the remaining canoeing of the Colorado."

The remaining time in the Colorado Canyon is spent splashing one another, having normal conversations they haven't had since no one remembers, and acting like a family again. Trevor was right about the time. After two hours of leisurely paddling, the canyon changes as does the scenery.

Entering Santa Elena Canyon, the canyon walls begin climbing to dizzying heights of up to 1500 feet. The walls are not smooth but rather carved out like one would take a chisel to a pile of chocolate. There is a soothing roughness that attracts small ferns and cottonwood tree samplings grasping hold as tightly as possible in order to survive. Starling nests are evident as they can be seen darting along the crevices and precipitous ledges lining the walls.

Trevor motions everyone over to the bank. "I think it is best for me to explain the different rapids we are about to encounter, and to get you ready mentally for what you are about to encounter. The Santa Elena rapids are somewhat bigger and faster, but very doable. As we enter this first rapid, follow me through the notch. Robbie, you'll need to paddle and steer at the same time, so watch what I do so you don't let the current take you where you don't want to be. As we get dumped out of the notch, we are going to paddle hard to our left. Terrence and Eleanor, you need to reach straight out to your left and pull as hard as you can perpendicular to the gun wall. Robbie, paddle on your right side as hard as you can so we can make it over the eddy created behind the huge rock on the left. Once there, we will begin stage 2. Follow me from there riding the current through the rapids, back paddling as you go. We'll be through the first rapid in no time. OK, push off from shore, and follow me through the notch, then to your left. Let's go."

"I don't know about this," Eleanor says with a reluctant sound in her voice.

"I told you, Mother, I will take care of you. That's my job right now. Let me worry about the both of us this time," Robbie tries to say in a reassuring voice. Eleanor nods just slightly enough for Robbie to notice. Robbie helps his mother in the canoe so she can situate herself in the bow seat while he pushes off then jumps in before getting his feet wet.

As they get closer to the first rapid, still one hundred yards away, Mrs. Jasper is very annoyed as to how much louder the roar is. "I can't believe how noisy this next rapid is. It truly sounds like a freight train. I'm scared. I don't know how I'm going to do this."

"Honey, I know you can do this. It's going to take more energy and mental toughness to go through these next set of rapids. You just have to do it. I know you can," Mr. Jasper says reassuringly.

"I guess. Robbie, honey, you will keep me safe, won't you?" "Of course, Mother. Listen to my instructions, and we'll wind up having a great time when it's all over," Robbie says. As they get closer, the roar gets so much louder. It's almost deafening. Robbie can see his Mother say something, but the roar of the rapids drowns out everything she is trying say. Now, he's worried. How is he going to shout out instructions if she can't hear him? It's time. They are at the entrance to the rapids. The roar is deafening. Trevor spots the notch, and before Robbie realizes it, they are through it and paddling like hell to the left side. He sees his father reaching stroke after stroke, trying to guide their canoe out of the fast current toward that huge rock over on the left.

"I can do this. Just believe in yourself, and you can get it done," Robbie says under his breath. "Here we go, Mother. As soon as we clear

the notch, start reaching to your left, and don't stop until I get the canoe pointing in that direction. Do you hear me, Mother?"

"I only heard bits or what you were saying. I will try to do what your father was doing. Is that OK?" she shouts.

"I only heard bits of what you were saying. Here we go!" The current pulls them through the notch, and Mrs. Jasper makes a weak effort of reaching like what Robbie's father displayed. He realizes that he will have to do this all himself. He paddles like all get out on the right side, trying to turn the canoe against the fast current, but it just makes them go faster. Without his mother's help to turn the canoe against the current, this is not going to work.

"We're not going to make it," Robbie shouts to the wind. "We're not going to make it!"

He realizes he will have to guide them through the rest of the rapids without knowing what stage 2 is. Since his mother can't hear any directions he shouts to her, it is up to him to get them through It's obvious his mother is clueless as to what she needs to do. Whatever she tries to do with her oar isn't working. He back paddles on the left to get them turned around one rock in the middle of the rapid, but he doesn't have enough time by himself to get them turned around an even bigger rock just past that one. As Robbie maneuvers around that first rock, Trevor and Mr. Jasper watch in horror as Robbie's canoe hits it broadside. In just a few seconds, the strength of the rapids begin to bend the canoe in half. Robbie jumps out of his seat and jumps the length of the canoe to where his mother is seated. He lifts her up off the seat, and they scurry on top of the huge rock, all the while witnessing the power of the river bending their canoe in half. Mrs. Jasper is terrified beyond belief, not understanding what just happened or why. As she sits down on the huge rock, she begins to sob. Robbie tries to comfort her, but whatever he tries doesn't work. He just lets her cry and get it out her system.

Just then, Robbie sees Trevor's canoe launch from the eddy toward them. Since Mr. Jasper has the power to reach and make a difference in controlling the canoe, they finally maneuver around the first rock they encounter and around the rock where they are standing and into its eddy behind them.

There, Mr. Jasper grabs the rock for support while they all ponder what to do next.

"My wife needs to get to shore. I have to get her out of here. She's terrified," Mr. Jasper pleads.

"I agree, Terrence. Will you please stand up and climb to the top of the rock? I can hold the canoe steady in the eddy. Here, I have a rope behind my seat you can tie to your support and hold onto it to keep our canoe positioned here," Trevor says.

Terrence gets out of the canoe and scales the top of the rock. "Honey, sweetheart, I have to get you out of here. Please let me help you get in the canoe so Trevor can take you to safety."

After a little coxing, Terrence is able to get Eleanor to climb down the rock backward, into the canoe, and Trevor heads to shore, which is just fifteen feet away. Slowly and carefully, he escorts her out of the canoe to shore where she sits on a comfortable looking rock and continues to cry some more.

While still holding the canoe to the boulder, he looks over to his wife, and she is filled with complete distress and sadness as he witnesses his wife balling her head off. He knows there is nothing he can do at the moment. All he wants to do is get off this blasted rock and comfort his wife.

"Terrence, I have an idea how we can free the canoe. With the rope I'm going to throw you, tie it off like you did ours. As I make my way upstream with the rope, you and Robbie push as hard as you can on the other side. That should free it so I can pull it to shore!" Trevor yells over the roaring water. "What about the supplies and our clothes?" Terrence yells back.

"They will be lost, but we might be able to catch up with them downstream. Let's start with freeing the canoe first. Ready?"

"Yes. We're in position."

Robbie and his father inch themselves down the huge rock where they can leverage to push the canoe out on one side. As they grunt and moan and Trevor pulls on the rope, to their amazement, the canoe begins to budge.

"Pull harder, Trevor!" Terrence shouts. "Push harder, Terrence. Don't stop!"

Their efforts are fruitful. The crumpled canoe is dislodged, and Trevor pulls toward him through the gushing water what once looked like a canoe. He finally gets it to shore ten minutes later since fighting the current makes slow headway. Trevor walks his canoe upstream so he can paddle down to where the two remain on the rock. With the supplies emptied out of the canoe, Trevor is able to get both of them off the huge rock and to shore safely where Mrs. Jasper is sitting. She has at least stopped crying, but is completely terrified. Terrence ventures to where she is sitting and keeps her company, hugging and caressing her for reassurance.

"Father, how's Mother doing?" Robbie asks.

"Not good, son. She needs time and reassurance," Terrence says. "We'll know in a little while after she has had time to gather herself."

"What can I do, Terrence?" Trevor asks.

"I don't know if there's anything anyone can do right now. I'll know better later," Terrence replies. "We won't get very far in just one canoe. What's going to happen?"

"What do you mean, just one canoe? I'll have this one seaworthy in no time!" Trevor says astonishingly.

"How?" Terrence asks. "It's ruined. It doesn't even look like a canoe anymore. I don't know what it looks like. Perhaps, a pile of junk."

"Just watch," Trevor says. Trevor grabs the clothes bags from one canoe, places them on opposite sides to keep the canoe in place. To everyone's amazement, he does something no one thought was possible. He starts jumping up and down on top of it. Bouncing as much as two to three feet in the air. After a dozen or so jumps, something miraculous happens. The bent in half canoe begins moving. It slowly begins to take shape again, and within five minutes, the piece of junk looks like a canoe again, except for the huge scrape mark on the bottom where it was pinned against the huge rock.

"Incredible. I would have never guessed this could happen if I didn't see it for myself. Anything broken?" Robbie asks in amazement.

"No, nothing broken," Trevor replies. "How was that possible?" Terrence asks.

"Do you remember how I described these canoes at the beginning of your trip?" Trevor asks.

"Yeah. You said they were indestructible. You made me a believer," Robbie says.

"Me, too," Terrence replies.

"Terrence, we are going to move your wife just a short ways downstream where there is open area, flat ground to make camp, and search for our supplies. In fact, they probably washed to shore already. After we load up one canoe with its supplies, Robbie, would you please come with me so we can find the other supplies? Terrence, please put your wife in your canoe and follow me very carefully. Eleanor clings tightly to Terrence sniffing and shaking as he slowly walks her to the canoe. Once Eleanor is safely situated in the bow, Terrence pushes off and jumps in without getting wet. We're past the worst of the rapids, so pull ashore about eighty yards downstream. We'll come back up to you after we find the other supplies," Trevor says.

"Honey, you wait here while I load our canoe, then I am going to take you to a safer place where you can rest. Can I do anything else for you?" Terrence asks.

"No, Terrence. You do what you need to do, then I'll be ready to go with you. I just need to lie down and rest. I'm still shaken up a lot," Eleanor says.

"Give me just a few minutes, then we are going to follow Trevor downstream to our campsite."

After loading the one canoe, Terrence follows Trevor and Robbie past a few more small rocks, which then flattens out into smoother water. He heads to shore while Robbie and Trevor continue downstream. "Honey, we're here. I'll help get you out of the canoe," Terrence says.

"Terrence, Robbie and I will be back shortly once we have loaded up the remaining supplies," Trevor says. "Robbie, you ready to go?"

"Let's head out so we can get back as soon as possible."

They push off from shore and head downstream. Not far away, Robbie sees a group of supplies scattered along the shoreline. "That must be our stuff," Robbie says. "Has anything like this happened before with you?"

"Yes, but not that often. Your mother will be fine by tomorrow morning, and we can get underway."

They inspect the supplies—nothing is broken or came open. "Let's load up these supplies and get back to your parents," Trevor says.

After loading up the supplies, Trevor and Robbie find the water is slack enough that they are able to paddle back to Mr. and Mrs. Jasper.

Upon arriving, Trevor says, "While you two set up camp along with your tents, I am going to get supper started. I think a jug of wine is called for after what happened today. It is safe to say that we are alive and safe. Eleanor, I don't want you to do anything except rest once Terrence has your tent set up. Rest all you want. You'll be better in the morning."

As Robbie and his father set up the tents, unroll the sleeping bags, and inspect the recovered supplies, Eleanor sits and rests while Trevor works on making supper.

"Trevor, do you mind if I have some wine now?" Eleanor asks. "Not at all. Help yourself."

"I want to apologize for my weakness. I had no idea I would behave like this," Eleanor explains through her sobbing. "Eleanor, please listen to me. You have just experienced a life-changing event, something you may never experience again. Your mind, as well as your body, is in mild shock because of it. You don't have to apologize for anything, or to me. I see people from all walks of life float this river not knowing what to expect until it slaps them in their faces. You have to deal with what happened in your own way. I will keep you safe and give you advice as much as I can. That is my job. You rest now, and we won't leave until you are good and ready. Does that help?" Trevor says.

"Yes, thank you very much. I don't want to hold up anyone. I hope I'll be ready to go again in the morning."

"We'll see, and I hope so also. You'll be better off once you decide to continue," Trevor says. "Hey, guys, supper is ready.

There are logs left over from the last group who came through that make great seats. Terrence ushers Eleanor to the most comfortable looking one, then sits beside her. "Do things like this happen very often," Terrence asks Trevor.

"Not very often, but I have seen worse." "How worse?"

"I have seen people freeze up for no reason at all. Their canoes wind up against a rock like yours did, but not everyone makes it out."

"You mean to tell me there are deaths that happen on this river." "I would be dishonest if I did not be truthful with you.

Yes, their are deaths on occasion."

With surprising information, everyone falls silent while finishing up dinner.

I think we should all get to bed early tonight, then shove off at a good time in the morning after breakfast. Tomorrow will be better. I know it," Trevor says.

CHAPTER ELEVEN

A s morning arrives, Robbie is the first one awake while Trevor is making breakfast. While they are talking, Terrence is awoken by the smell of coffee and their conversations.

Terrence checks on Eleanor, and she is sleeping very silently. He slowly and carefully inches himself out of the sleeping bag trying not to awaken her. After being successful, he quietly slips into his clothes, moves to the zipper door of the tent on his knees, unzips it ever so smoothly, exits the tent still on his knees, turns around and zips the tent flap behind him.

"Hey, that smells good. I will really miss that smell when we leave. It's better than any alarm clock," Terrence says.

"How is Eleanor doing, Terrence?" Trevor asks.

"Much better. I'll let her sleep a little while longer," Terrence replies. As they sit down and eat, Robbie says to Trevor, "I thought there would be more people camped out with us or still on the river."

"A lot of canoeing trips in the Santa Elena Canyon are based on one- day excursions. A few will continue through the canyon into Mariscal Canyon. But you're right. There should be some people in here already. Maybe they will show up shortly. I think Eleanor should be woken up so she can eat and get back some of her strength," Trevor says.

As Terrence finishes his breakfast, he walks up to his tent. All the commotion has awaken her, and she begins to stir in her sleeping bag. Terrence sits down besides her and says, "Did you sleep well, Honey. Do you think you feel well enough to get up and have some breakfast?"

"Yes, dear. I don't want to be the broken spoke in our adventure. I'm ready to get up and eat something." With Terrence's help, Eleanor rises out of her sleeping bag, puts on her clothes for the day, then climbs out of the tent.

"It's good to see you up and walking. How do you feel this morning?" Trevor asks.

"Much better, Trevor. You were right. I had to recover in my own way, and lots of rest seemed to do the trick. I'll take some of that delicious coffee."

The four of them sit around the fire enjoying coffee, eggs, bacon, biscuits, and beans. Things appear to be back to normal for another day on the river. There's not a breath of wind. Low hanging clouds about one-third from the top of the 1,500-foot cliffs begin to thin out. As they all continue feasting the delicious breakfast Trevor assembled for them, Eleanor hears something in the distance upriver and says, "Where is that roar coming from? We came through those rapids yesterday, and that noise wasn't there last night."

"The river can fluctuate from one day to the next. A little bit of rising water can make that sound," Trevor explains.

A breeze can be felt on everyone's faces, and Eleanor's hair begins to rustle. A minute later, the roar gets louder. Another minute later, it's even louder then. Robbie finally says, "I don't think the sudden change in the river's sound is normal. Something's not right."

Trevor didn't care to elaborate. He just listened. No more than a minute later, his eyes get huge, and Robbie notices the fear in them. He jumps up immediately and says, "You all have thirty seconds to grab whatever is important to you, throw it in the canoes, and we need to get the hell out of here, and I mean right now."

Disbelief and confusion strike everyone. No one moves.

They just look at one another.

"Come on!" Trevor demands. "Get off your butts now!

We have to leave right now!"

That finally got everyone moving. Eleanor and Terrence are rustling through their tent as if a bear got caught inside. Robbie is stuffing clothes in his waterproof bag. Trevor is throwing his kitchen supplies loosely into the canoe, then ripping down his tent.

"OK, time's up. Throw your stuff in the canoes right now. Push off, and let's go."

"Trevor, what's wrong? What's going on?" Terrence is shouting in disbelief.

"No time to explain until we get a ways downriver. Just trust me, we have to stay focused and get out of here," Trevor demands.

Eleanor is ranting and raving as Terrence paddles hard downriver. Trevor and Robbie make great time as both paddle hard straight down the middle. Their paddling is so in synch with one another that they are already twenty yards ahead Robbie becomes very concerned with his parents and how they are doing canoeing together that he looks back for a few seconds noticing his Father trying to say something The roar is so loud now that Trevor can't hear Terrence yell to him Just as soon as he yells one last time to Trevor about not looking back, the five-foot wall of rushing water overtakes the Jasper's canoe just as it hits the haystack Like a pencil, their canoe is thrust up into the air ten feet Luckily, their canoe doesn't turn to the side, and they land upright back on the rushing water. Robbie looks back again. Their few seconds of security is ended when their canoe plunges bow first into the water, tips end over end, and submerges. The canoe turns over and makes its way back up to the surface like the floating canoe it is, but without its occupants. Eleanor and Terrence are completely lost in the rushing water, never to be seen again. Robbie yells at the top of his lungs, "Mother, Father, where are you. Don't leave me alone. Show yourselves. I can't be without you. Show yourselves."

Fifteen seconds later, the wall of rushing water hits Trevor's canoe. They are also thrust into the air six feet to the left and also tilt to the left. Robbie is thrown out, and Trevor is able to gain control as the rushing water pushes him into the edge of a car-sized rock partially submerged. His canoe then flips over and is engulfed by the rush of water. The canoe gets tossed and turned by the water and debris until it hits another boulder, is trapped, and disappears under the torrent.

CHAPTER TWELVE

J udd Henson arrives in Lajitas in his open-air jeep wearing his normal Park Service attire and wide-brimmed hat that serves as a huge sunshade in the sweltering heat as well as an efficient umbrella when it does rain. His huge six-foot-three- inch frame and well-manicured mustache exits the jeep and walks toward the guide vendors. All the vendors are busy with people lined up for their river trips. Many are trying on life jackets and look like bumblebees walking around in circles, like they are drunk or something. With a slight wind in the air, dust is kicked up with every step. The tour guides know his reputation. There is nothing to find out from him unless he has something to say. His direct manner and firm voice is well respected. The report of the missing occupants from Trevor's river trip was reported to him four days ago. No one has been allowed on the river since then until it has finally been classified as post flood stage. Surprisingly, he walks past Southwest Texas Outfitters, Trevor's employer, down toward the river, then turns right upriver. Debris and broken trees are strewn all along the bank more than seven feet high into the native vegetation. It's a mile walk along the bank until he reaches his destination.

A small camp set up with very used tents of different colors resembles a miner's camp, unkept and untidy. A smoldering fire indicates that a meal was just finished and it was left alone to go out by itself. Woven lawn chairs with broken straps is the common decor by each tent. There's no one to be seen, which means the occupants must be taking naps. The temperature is not hot, yet, but it could easily get that way in no time. Judd was thinking that it would be nice to take a nap right now. Of course, that would completely be irresponsible and would sour his reputation. As he walks among the tents looking for life, he begins yelling into each one, "ST, where are you? It's Judd. Come on out. I need to talk to you. You are the only one who can help me."

"What do you mean I'm the only one who can help you? There are plenty of river guides to do your business. Why interrupt my life of luxury for something anyone else can do?" he shouts back through the tent.

"You know very well what I mean. All the other guides are full with trips, and no one is going to reschedule their trips for a wild goose hunt, especially when everyone knows there's no chance of finding anyone alive. Today is the first day allowing trips on the river since the flood incident, and everyone is excited to start making money again. I don't see anyone lined up to do business here. So please, come out so we can talk," Judd pleads.

The tent flap slowly opens, and what emerges only slightly resembles a human. The thin but muscular figure has dirty blond hair hanging halfway down its back. The remaining hair completely hides a face that looks like it was last washed a few months ago. The thick blond mustache hanging over the upper lip moves with every word. The ragged and dirty sleeveless shirt is a solid bland gray, and the blue jean shorts covering thin, muscular legs are kept up with a tattered leather belt.

"All right, Judd. Now that you have awoken me from my mansion, what's so important that only I can help?" ST asks uninterestingly.

"The lost occupants from Trevor's trip. I want you to find their bodies, or at least what may be left of them," Judd asks. "Take either FAM or Hooty with you, but not DBoR. They're not good for anything else except ballast and another pair of hands for paddling. Besides, another set of eyes might be of help."

"You know, if you offer any of the other guides double booking, they just might consider doing it for you."

"I don't want any tour guide. I want you. You know this river better than anyone I have met. You know how it changes from one day to the next and what to expect. With pressure mounting from the Park Service headquarters to find something concrete in which to report to the next of kin, I want only the best, and, ST, you know you are the best. Right?"

Judd kisses ass for a positive reply.

"I won't charge you double booking like the tour groups would, but I will charge hazard pay and expenses," ST replies. "I can probably get under way as soon as I prepare my seal- tight meals and booze."

"Hey, no booze. I'm not paying for your booze," Judd scolds.

"I always pack booze on all my trips. You know that. In fact, the tourists expect it."

"Fine, but no hard stuff. I want you lucid and focused on this trip."

"Agreed," ST complies. "Give me a half day, and I can be halfway through the Colorado before nightfall. I can make it to where the haystack hit them within two days. From there, I may wind up in the Mariscal. I'll have a guide service notify you as to my location when I emerge from the river and have something to report."

"Sounds good. I'm depending on you, ST. This is important," Judd says.

"Yeah, yeah. Talk to you in a few," ST replies. ST gets busy right away, setting up his canoe with equipment and kitchen supplies, and gets to work making meals for three to four days on the river, and of course, stowing booze.

"Hooty, did you get all the kitchen supplies packed and secure?" ST asks.

"Yeah, boss. No worries. Hey, how long do you think we'll be?" "Depends on what we find, and how far the flood surge pushed their bodies downstream. We may have to go through the Mariscal, and even into Boquillas, but I hope the boulders and other obstacles will collect whatever went downstream from the incident site. We'll just have to see once we get there. If we maintain hard paddling until nightfall, I'm hoping to get through most of the Colorado by tonight. Let's go, buddy," ST says.

As they push off with a canoe full of supplies—and booze, of course—ST maintains a pace only race competitors could appreciate. As predicted, ST and Hooty make it halfway through the Colorado by dusk. "OK, Hooty, we're pulling in over there. We need to make a fire for supper and get our tents set up before it gets too dark. I figure we have about half an hour before the sun escapes below the canyon walls," ST says. When they beach the canoe, Hooty knows the routine well. He throws the watertight bags and tent supplies up on shore. He immediately rolls out the tent, gets it set up, then the sleeping bags. All the while, ST gathers driftwood left over from the floodwaters, starts a fire, and starts warming up the seal-tight bags of food in hot water. To the side of the hot water pots, he throws on a couple of chicken thighs. "Hey, boss, when can we break into the booze?" Hooty shouts from inside the tent.

"What do you want, buddy? Beer or tequila? "I'll start with beer for now."

"OK, but make sure you pace yourself. I don't want to scrape you off the beach again like I did last time. You were wiped out for the entire next day, and I need you sharp. Got it?" ST orders.

"Got it. If I start stuttering, you can throw me in the tent so I can sleep it off," Hooty announces.

"You be responsible for yourself. If you start stuttering, you'll wind up in the river," ST replies.

Hooty just stands there, staring as if surprised by ST's remarks. It finally hits home to him when he blinks several times in rapid succession. "I get your drift."

"When I first found you, you and FAM were just wandering about, clueless and nowhere to go. I have seen you change these past few years, Hooty, and I can only hope to see you change some more. Give me the benefit of the doubt by staying sharp tomorrow and helping me find those poor souls that got caught in the horrendous surge. Can you do that for me?" ST asks.

"I don't know where I'd be without you, boss. Throw me in the river if you have to tonight. I promise you I'll be sharp and won't let you down," Hooty says.

"Good. Let's enjoy the night together. Tomorrow, we get back to business. I'll start with some tequila and chase it later with beer."

Eating and drinking in good company consumed half the night. There wasn't a cloud in the night sky, and the Milky Way exhibited itself in full glory. The canyon walls allow only six to eight hours of sunlight, and even fewer in Santa Elena with 1,500-foot-high walls. ST and Hooty were up by six thirty the next morning making a fire to fix breakfast.

"What'd you pack for breakfast, boss?" Hooty asks. "Normal stuff. Eggs, bacon, biscuits, and beans. Help yourself. We're going to paddle hard all day to reach the Matadero Rapids before nightfall where the incident happened. I'm hoping we'll find something between there and the False Sentinel Rapids," ST says. "If we're lucky, the boulders and other obstacles will catch what we want to find."

CHAPTER THIRTEEN

T hey both paddle hard all day like ST said and make it to the headwaters of the Matadero Rapids. "Great job, Hooty I'm proud of you. You stayed with it all day. Can't tell you how much you have improved. If you keep this up, you'll have to come up a different name for yourself," ST says in delight. "With limited daylight left, let's camp here on the flats and get started in the morning. Be honest with you, Hooty, I'm not looking forward to what we may find tomorrow."

"That goes for me, too, boss. How about no drinking tonight?" "Once again, I'm proud of you. Good advice. Let's get camp set up and eat some chow, then make it an early night," ST says.

As they go through the routine to set up camp and get supper started, not much is spoken. The time spent before they hit the sack is rather solace. The reality of what they might see and experience tomorrow occupies their thoughts and fears.

Morning arrives with an overcast sky, but to their benefit, the cloud cover is just above the steep canyon walls. As they both emerge from the tent, ST says, "Looks like a dreary day for a dreary job. Break camp while I get breakfast started, Hooty."

"Right, boss. Just want to get this over with. Hope we find something quickly. Don't want to drag this out," Hooty exclaims.

"I'm with you, buddy. Eat up well. We may have a long day ahead of us," ST replies.

They load up the canoe after breaking camp. They paddle hard to get to the middle of the river. As they near the rapids, they shoot the notch right of center. ST paddles hard on the right while Hooty reaches to his left. As they fight the current, they make it to the eddy behind the boulder on the left. While they gather themselves, ST back strokes hard on the left quickly turning the canoe around one-eighty. As the current catches them, they fight to avoid the wall of rocks jetting out one-third of the way on the left, aiming for the notch next to a huge boulder on the right. They get near the notch at a forty-five degree angle—suicide if they hit the notch that way. In a desperation backstroke on his left, ST is able to straighten out the canoe just as they enter the fast-flowing water shooting them through the notch. As they shoot through, Hooty says, "I wonder if they made that one?" "No matter how busy we are fighting the current and finding our notches, keep your eyes peeled everywhere, even on the canyon walls for anything," ST orders.

The rest of the rapids is not bad to negotiate. They make it through fine and hit smooth water soon after. As they spy around them looking for any signs of the party, nothing shows up.

"Before we hit the False Sentinel Rapids a little ways downstream, there are haystacks to go through. If I'm right, I imagine the flood surge probably hit them just as they hit those haystacks. The ones in the first rapids are not bad, but these are worse. Those two- to two-and-a-half- foot haystacks could easily grow to over five to six feet. If that is what happened, their canoes could have become airborne, as much as twelve to fifteen feet. Hooty, as we pass the haystacks, that's when we need to start looking hard at everything. Got it, buddy?" ST says.

"Yeah, I got it. I won't let you down, boss."

ST pushes out the canoe into the current, heading straight toward the haystacks. They are three feet tall, normal size for most of them, then navigate toward the big boulder in front of them. ST paddles hard on the left side while Hooty reaches on his right. They safely make it to the eddy behind the boulder. "We're going to find every eddy we can to give us time to look at everything. Whatever happened probably happened around here, but we may not actually find anything for another hundred yards downstream. I don't want to miss anything," ST says.

ST back paddles hard on the right side, sending the canoe into the current. There's another huge boulder right in the middle of the river with fast water on both sides. However, the next notch after that is clear on the left side. ST paddles hard on the right side, trying to get around the huge boulder, but can't make it. Instead, he back paddles, sending the canoe straight into the right notch. The current shoots them through so fast, ST shouts, "Hooty, reach with all your might! Get us over there."

Hooty reaches repetitively like a machine as ST paddles on his right. The current is fast and pushing them parallel with the current. With both of them fighting as hard as they can, it's a wonder if Trevor's party made this at all. Glancing over his right shoulder and fighting the current, ST sees something long and blue submerged below the waterline up against a boulder. He exhales a great sigh because he now knows how far they got—or didn't.

"Come on, Hooty. Keep reaching. I'm depending on you, buddy!" ST has to shout.

With just a matter of feet of room left before hitting the notch, ST back paddles on his right, shooting them through the notch. "Just ahead of us, Hooty. Head for the eddy behind that boulder."

In no time, the current pushes them to the boulder. Hooty reaches once again on his left, and ST pushes on his right, turning the canoe on a dime and into the eddy. "I know now that they never made it this far. Whatever we find will be downstream from here," ST says in a solemn voice. "Let's catch our breath before exiting these rapids. We'll hit San Carlos Rapids next. We'll have time to spy around before that."

ST back paddles on his left, sending them into the current. Maneuvering around small rocks here and there is easy. There is one more sizable boulder on the left before exiting into smoother water. Hooty shouts above the roar of the rapids, "Boss, I see something. It's a red canoe submerged just below the waterline. Do you think it was theirs?"

"Yeah, probably. Haven't seen that before, so it must have been deposited recently. Hey, hit that eddy right now. I see something," ST demands.

Hooty reaches left hard while ST pushes on his right. They hit the eddy just before they get too far past the boulder to stop. "What do you see, boss?"

"Look up. Tell me what you see," ST says.

"Well, there's a small ledge about twenty feet up which is more than I can say for the rest of the canyon walls. Oh hey, I see something dangling over it," Hooty says excitedly.

"Good eyes, buddy. I knew you would be helpful. Now, how to get up there and check it out?"

"These walls are straight up. How do you suppose he got up there?" Hooty asks.

"I know the blue canoe met its demise when it hit that last haystack. The flood surge must have propelled the red canoe into the air over to the left, spilling its occupants. With the water level much higher than it is now, it's possible that this survivor made it to this boulder and scaled the walls to that ledge to safety. How he got up there, I have no idea. I do know that adrenaline can give people incomprehensible feats of strength. Give me a minute to think about what to do next."

After ST has a chance to catch his thoughts, he says, "Well, I don't like it, but I'm going to have to scale these walls with climbing ropes and see what's going on up there and whether or nor he is alive. Throw a lasso around this boulder, Hooty, holding us stationary. I don't want our canoe going anywhere once I start climbing," ST says.

Hooty finds a rope under his bow seat, makes a simple lasso, and casts it around the huge boulder. "OK, boss. Got it. Take off."

85

ST carefully places each foothold testing it with his body weight all the while, carrying a coil of climbing rope over his shoulder. Each and every step is carefully planned. He has climbing fingers—strong but nimble and able to grab hold of the smallest depression in the rock wall while supporting his weight as he finds a foothold. Minutes meld into half hours while ST carefully calculates each and every step. After what seems like several hours, ST finally reaches the overhang nearly forty- five minutes later. He inspects the survivor and yells down to Hooty, "We have a live one. I'm going to secure the rope with a stake and lower him down to you. Please place him in the canoe carefully and keep him comfortable until I get back down," ST instructs Hooty.

After hammering in the necessary supports to accommodate the weight of the survivor, ST lowers him down where Hooty is waiting in the canoe. While Hooty rests the survivor's head and covers him with a blanket, ST begins his descent trying to follow his very steps as he ascended the cliff wall. It takes ST at least twenty minutes to reach the canoe while trying not to make any disastrous mistakes on his way down. "Good job, Hooty. OK, let's get out of here. There are quite a few rapids to negotiate before finding a pull-out place. Let's go," ST advises.

The San Carlos and Entrance Rapids, which are classified as class II rapids, are easy to negotiate, especially with extra ballast in the canoe. All the while, ST keeps a vigilant eye on the survivor. They pass Entrance Camp, which is a clearing along the river bank just right for overnight camping. No one there. The next rapid, called Rock Slide Rapid, is classified as class III and is full of huge rocks the size of garages and cars. The water being squeezed through and around the rocks makes for fast shoots. "Hooty, there's not a lot of

86

cutbacks through Rock Slide, but we have to be sharp in order to find the notches we want. Be ready to switch hands on a second's notice," ST orders.

"Got it, boss. Just let me know what you want me to do, and I'll do it," Hooty replies.

Shooting the notch on the right, the fast water dumps them right in front of Castle Rock, which is a house-size boulder. Hitting that rock will be the end of them. "Hooty, reach left right now. Get us around this beast!" ST yells.

Hooty reaches left stroke after stroke while ST back paddles hard on the left, turning the canoe but still being at the mercy of the current. With a desperation stroke, ST pushes hard on the right, propelling them just within feet of the massive beast and sending them into the next notch.

"Good job, Hooty. The other notches are not difficult to get to, but stay sharp as I bolt out orders on which side I want you to reach!" ST shouts over the roar. "OK, Hooty, reach left!" That next notch is easy, sending them into open rushing water and leaving them enough room to get over to the right where the next notch is located. "Hooty, get over to the right!" While Hooty reaches right, ST paddles hard on the left, easily maneuvering them through the next notch. Each notch after that is left, another left, way right, through the middle, then finally to the right, spilling them into flat water.

"Way to keep us steady, Hooty. Let's rest for a minute before paddling hard again. I think that's the last of Classified Rapids, but we do have a series of small canyons to go through before our take-out," ST announces.

Once they begin their paddling cadence again, the slow current takes them through Fern Canyon, which is narrow but easy to negotiate. Next, they go past Smuggler's Cave, which is popular with hikers. Passing the Santa Elena confluence, their next stop just one hundred yards downstream is the Santa Elena River Access. Pulling out at the access, ST gives Hooty instructions to keep the survivor comfortable and hydrated. He exits the canoe and walks toward a group of people waiting around. "Excuse me, please. I have a survivor in my canoe from an accident upstream, and I would appreciate the use of one of your cell phones to contact the Park Service," ST asks.

"Judd, ST here. I'm at the Santa Elena River Access with a survivor. He needs immediate medical attention," ST says. "I'm on my way and will be there in thirty to forty minutes.

By the way, can you tell what condition he's in?" Judd asks. "He's bung up with bruises but no broken bones that I can see. I think he's actually in better condition than what I would expect considering what he has gone through. I know he's dehydrated and needs fluids fast," ST replies.

"Well, just keep him comfortable, then we'll take him to the hospital," Judd says.

"What do you mean we?" ST asks.

"You heard me right. I think he deserves to know his rescuers when he becomes stable. After that, I'll take you back to the access where you can continue downstream for the other occupants.

CHAPTER FOURTEEN

While ST and Hooty wait for Judd to arrive, a group of people mingle around their canoe. It's all they can do to keep them away while they monitor the survivor and keep him hydrated.

Judd finally arrives about forty minutes later, and ST is glad to get him in Judd's truck and en route to the hospital another thirty minutes away.

As they pull up, emergency personnel take away the survivor and do whatever they do to keep him alive. "Doctor, when can we see him to find out what happened?" Judd asks. "Don't know right now, but I would say that he is very fortunate to be alive as much as he is considering what he experienced," the doctor replies. "I'm hoping you can see him in less than an hour. I'll let you know."

Sitting in the waiting room, Judd asks ST, "Where'd you find him?"

"I think they all wiped out in the second set of rapids of the Matadero where the switchback to the next notch is clear across the river. The flood surge must have hit them just as they encountered the haystack, catapulting them airborne. Our guy was fortunate enough to make it to the next boulder

89

he hit, scale it, them climb twenty or so straight up the canyon wall to a small ledge that saved his life. It takes extraordinary strength to climb that vertical distance after being thrown around in the swelling current," ST says.

"He seems to be an extraordinary survivor, not having any broken bones or serious cuts and scrapes. Can't wait to talk to this guy," Judd says.

"I'll tell you one thing—I would not have made it without Hooty's help. He was great. I can see why the lost party did not make it very far. The current changed some, and I think Trevor was not aware of the complete inexperience of some of the occupants," ST replies.

As they wait a little while later, the doctor announces that the survivor is lucid enough for visitors. Entering the ER room and seeing the survivor with IVs and hoses coming out of him everywhere, Judd eases up to him. Holding his right hand, Judd says softly, "Son, my name is Judd Henson, and I work for the Park Service. I'm glad to see you are doing well and in good condition. Do you know your name?"

His mouth flutters up and down as if he is trying to say something. Obviously, it must be difficult for him to move anything, including his mouth. Stuttering, the words come out, "R-R-R-Robbie J-J-J-Jasper."

"That's right. You are Robbie Oliver Jasper, and your parents are Terrence and Eleanor."

"W-W-W-Where are my parents?"

"We are still looking for them, but believe me, we will find them," Judd says hesitantly. "Who saved me?"

"This gentleman right behind me. His name is ST." "S-S-S-S T-T-T, thank you, sir. What do you do?"

"I was hired by Judd here to find you and your party," ST says softly. "I mean, what do you do?" Robbie asks demandingly. "I'm a river guide. I'm a river rat. I live on the river."

A slow but distinct smile forms on Robbie's face, "What about my parents? Are they here, too?"

"We are still looking for them, son."

"What does that mean, still looking for them?"

The doctor quietly ushers then out of the room. Tears fill Robbie's eyes as he sulks, then he loses conciseness.

"OK, guys, that's enough for now. Judd, I'll keep you posted as to his condition, but I don't think he'll be in any condition for interviews for quite some time. I think his shock from the accident is finally taking its toll," the Doctor says.

"ST, I'll take you back to the river access so you can continue your search downstream. I'm hoping you won't have to go any farther than the

Mariscal. I'll wait to hear from you. Thank you very much for what you have done so far. This guy really needed you, and you came through with flying colors," Judd says.

"Thanks, Judd. I guess it's time to go. Can't wait to get back," ST replies.

CHAPTER FIFTEEN

J udd shows up at the hospital. After checking in with the nurse's station, he asks to speak with Dr. Zisk who treated Robbie when he was admitted the day before. When Dr. Zisk finally arrives, Judd says, "Well doctor, how is our patient doing today?" "Physically, he's doing great.

The next morning, the doctor shows up to check up on Robbie. While examining Robbie, Dr. Zisk notices his eyes are full of tears. "Is there anything you want to talk about, son?"

Without raising his head or making any motion at all, Robbie gently shakes his head to the side once. "That's alright, son. I'll give you some more time and check in on you later."

When Dr. Zisk looks in on Robbie after lunch, he notices his lunch hasn't been touched. "Robbie, I am terribly sorry about what happened, and I want you to know how sorry I am about your loss. I also know you would like more time to mourn your parents. There are some things that have started in motion that you need to know about. After making a few decisions, you can find a more appropriate time to mourn your parents.

"Robbie, Judd Henson forwarded to me your grandparents' contact information, and I have notified them as to your condition. Since you will be released this afternoon, they are on their way from Muncie, Indiana, to collect you," Dr. Zisk says.

"Since I turned eighteen a few months ago, am I legally able to make my own decision?" Robbie inquires.

"Yes, son, you are. Are you saying you don't want your grandparents to get you?"

"I'm not sure I have much of a life to go back to. I want very much to mourn my parents in the proper way, but for right now, I want to talk to one person before I make that decision. His answer will determine what decision I make after that," Robbie replies. "Please call Judd Henson to come here and pick me up. I want to explain everything to him, and him only."

"I don't understand what you are doing, son, but I will respect your wishes. I'll have him here by afternoon," Dr. Zisk says.

"Thank you, Doc. Please let me know when he gets here."

As Judd Henson arrives at the hospital, Dr. Zisk meets him outside Robbie's room. "Judd, Robbie says he wants to talk to only one person, and the answer he receives will determine what he does. I can only assume that person is you."

"Well, I guess we'll find out together. How is he doing?" He still has a lot of emotions inside of him that need to come out before he can properly heal, and that will happen in time. Otherwise, he's doing much better.

"Much better. I am releasing him today as long as he has a place to go to," Dr. Zisk says.

"OK, Doc, here we go," Judd says.

As they both enter Robbie's room, he says, "Glad to see you again, Mr. Henson."

"Judd, just call me Judd."

"Judd, I want to talk to someone who will help me determine my fate and what I choose to do before leaving Big Bend. Will you please take me back to Lajitas?" Robbie asks.

Judd looks at Dr. Zisk in amazement with a confused look on his face. "Why Lajitas?" Judd asks in bewilderment.

"Please. No more questions until we get there."

"You have us all dumbstruck, Robbie. Who is in Lajitas?" Judd ponders.

Robbie just stares at them without another word. "Dr. Zisk, can Robbie be released to me?" Judd asks.

"Yes, Judd, as long as you take responsibility for him until he makes his decision. Robbie, I'll have you processed, then you can leave with Judd. Judd, will you please wait in the Lobby until Robbie is ready to go?" Dr. Zisk asks.

Judd is completely perplexed, and it shows on his face like a bad poker hand. Robbie arrives in the Lobby and says, "Ready to go. I want to get out of here."

"Are you going to tell me what this is all about?" Judd asks demandingly.

"Yes, I will. Especially because you deserve it, but not until we get there."

The ride back to Lajitas is silent since no one knows what else to talk about. Pulling up to the city limits, Judd asks, "OK. Now where?"

"Please park anywhere along the river trip vendors. I'm getting out, and I would appreciate it if you will take me to ST."

"ST? Why ST?"

"You'll find out when we get there. Please, Judd, it is very important." "All right. I guess everyone is going to be surprised with what you have to say," Judd answers.

They make their way past the river tour vendors, down toward the river, turn right, then walk the mile to ST's camp. "I don't think you are going to like what you will see. He and his friends live a squandered life. Nothing to write home about," Judd says.

Robbie says nothing but just keeps walking. As they walk around a small bend in the river, there lies a small camp with very used tents of different colors. Two people are sitting around a fire sitting in dilapidated lawn chairs. One of them gets up slowly as if not being used to seeing strangers. "Hey, FAM. How's it hanging? Where's ST?" Judd asks.

"That piece of shit is still in his tent. Just got back from that wild goose hunt you sent him on. You have no idea what condition those other people were—"

Judd interrupts immediately and says, "Stop right there.

Don't say another word. You got me?" FAM shuts up and just nods in confusion. Judd makes his way over to ST's tent. "ST? You in there?"

"Is that you, Judd. Go away. No more favors. Just want to relax for the rest of the month. I went all the way to Boquillas before calling you. What else do you want?"

"There's someone here who wants to talk to you," Judd says.

"Who wants to talk to me? You're the only one I talk to besides Rachael at the guide service when they are all overbooked," ST answers.

"Come on out and meet the survivor whose life you saved." As ST emerges from his tent, his appearance has not changed. Still the same dirty long blond hair hanging halfway down his back, a thick blond mustache hanging over the upper lip rustling with every breath, bland gray shirt with the sleeves missing, and blue jean shorts held up with the same worn leather belt.

ST graciously walks up to Robbie to shake his hand. "It's a pleasure to see you in such better condition."

"I owe you my thanks, gratitude, and my life. No one in my entire life has done much for me except tell me what to do all the time. I want to know more about the person who braved the Rio Grande to find me," Robbie says. "By the way, my name is Robbie Jasper, Robbie *Oliver* Jasper."

"Robbie Oliver Jasper, hmmm, ROJ," ST says.

A smirk appears on Robbie's face as if in agreement. "I'm sorry. What did you say?"

"ROJ. Everyone here has a nickname because everyone has voluntarily abandoned their former lives to be here. If you are here on any other capacity besides demonstrating your thanks for my saving your life, your name will be ROJ," ST says.

"Who's everyone else?" Robbie asks.

"The person who met you when you arrived here is FAM. She has a filthy-ass mouth and is not allowed to speak to our guests or clients. She is, however, a good cook and keeps us all fed. Hooty, my companion who helped save you as well, showed up one day with FAM just wandering around not knowing where to go or what to do. They were two out-of- luck cases whose car broke down just outside of Lajitas. I took them in. He said he didn't give a hoot about anything or anyone at the time, so the name stuck. DBoR, over there, doing nothing at the moment, is the muscle of the group. He's also good fixing things as long as he is shown what to do. Otherwise, he's dumb as a box of rocks."

FAM is of normal height, on the skinny side because of an overactive metabolism, straight brown hair down to her shoulders but has thinned out because of bad eating habits.

Hooty, is slightly taller than she, but not by much. He also has brown hair that is straight, and he has been growing it out since he hasn't had money lately to get it cut. Since he also has a thin frame, both their clothes hang off their bodies in a very loose fashion. They both left the slums of Chicago looking for something more. One day, they decided to take her car and just drive. It took them as far as Lajitas, Texas where it broke down outside of town. DBoR is muscular in nature and has only a few shirts and pants to his name. He's a local Texan who got separated from his tour group. ST realized right away his unintelligible nature when he spied him wandering around town not knowing the name of his group or when they left. ST took him in and has been somewhat of a guardian to him ever since.

"Before I answer you, what does ST mean?"

"Judd, you want to answer ROJ's question?" ST says. "Every time I ever needed something—a river trip for a group of tourists who show up without reservations, or when the river tour vendors are overbooked and need someone to accommodate them—ST is always a sure thing. That's how the name stuck."

"Thank you for explaining that to me. Now, to answer your question. I, too, have no life to go back to. This is what I want. I want to be a river rat and learn your trade, live free, and make my own choices for a change," Robbie says sternly.

"Robbie, please reconsider," Judd demands.

"Judd, I want to thank you for all your help, and I hope to see you many times again. This is my decision. I want to be a river rat. That's final. If anyone inquires about me or my whereabouts, tell them I am out of touch for the time being." "I'll keep an eye on you for a while. ST, I'm looking to you to keep him safe and healthy. Will you do that for me?"

Judd asks. "Sure thing."

CHAPTER SIXTEEN

O K, kid, I mean, ROJ, if you want to be a river rat, you'll need your own tent and supplies. Let's take a canoe ride into town at the outfitters. They'll have everything you could possibly want and more. Don't go hog wild because you still have to pay me back once you have guided your first river trip. That will come in time. When we get back with your stuff, we'll go over a lot more.

After stocking up at the outfitters, ROJ carries everything in a huge duffel bag over his shoulders down to the canoe. "Throw everything in. We have a mile to go. You'll learn to use muscles you never had. Since we have time, what's your story?" ST asks.

"What do you mean, what's my story?"

"There's a reason why you chose to be here," ST says.

As ROJ contemplates ST's question, a flood of emotions invade his thoughts. As he remembers how his parents were thrown from their canoe and lost forever, he fights back tears even though he knows his eyes are glazing over. He can barely come to grips with explaining what happened. Since ST is going to be an important part of his life now, he deserves to know. Tightening his throat and calming his demeanor, ROJ is able to respond.

"My parents brought me on a ten-day river trip down the Rio Grande as part of my high school graduation and to become closer as a family. Growing up and being told what to do all the time and having my life planned out for me, I'm glad to be on my own for a change. That's all there is," ROJ says.

"I know there has to be more to it than that, but that's OK. You'll talk about it when you're ready. You just lost your parents, and I know it takes time to recover from that," ST replies.

"Yes, ST, there is more to it than that. You are very observant and smart. I'll be glad to tell you all about it when the time comes. I just want to start my new life here with you and learn as much as I can. That's what I'm excited about right now," ROJ firmly says.

"We're almost home. I'll show you how to set up your tent and get situated. When you have relaxed, we'll get started with everything," ST says. "FAM, when do you want us to eat lunch?" ST shouts.

"Keep your panties on, Your Highness. Lunch will be ready in ten!"FAM shouts back.

"What ever you do, ROJ, don't talk to her unless you want to be insulted. That's her way of communicating," ST says.

FAM prepared a simple lunch consisting of pork and beans and PB&J sandwiches followed by chocolate bars for dessert. "That was great, FAM. Everything tastes great prepared outdoors," ROJ says politely. "Well, get used to it because everything is prepared outdoors." "Hooty, show ROJ where we keep all the river trip supplies. He needs to get started right away," ST says.

"Right away, boss. ROJ, follow me. Your apprenticeship starts now," Hooty says.

Hooty takes ROJ to a makeshift plastic hut constructed out of used blue containers. They have been cut and put together with leather stitching. Inside, there are neatly assembled piles of plastic bags, weathertight containers and bags, and dry and canned food items. "ST is going to take you on a five-day river trip through the upper canyons. Grab whatever food you would like to eat, and I'll show you how to cook and bag it to be eaten later. I will get the wine. Don't want you to accidentally trip and break any of it. ST is really sensitive to that."

"In order to save room and weight, all canned foods are opened and put into plastic bags to be heated later. With the skillets already on the fire, cook the Salisbury streak, then the pork chops in mushroom soup. While that's going on, marinade the chicken in salad dressing seasoning.

This will keep it nice and moist until you cook it. Start making sandwiches with PB&J and cold cut meats and cheese. Bag those, as well. Once the food is prepared, you'll pick up ice in town and put everything in these Igloos. The wine goes in its separate containers. You'll be surprised how simple meals prepared well and with love will taste so good. OK, you're done here. Go see what ST wants you to do next," Hooty says.

"Done with the food, ST. What's next?" ROJ asks. "Good job. Bring everything down to the canoes, and I'll show you how to pack a canoe."

Dragging 250 pounds down to the river takes several trips. "Now, watch closely. If you pack a canoe wrong, the shifting weight will capsize it in no time. The heavy Igloos go in the middle. Everything else goes around it. You can pack your own canoes the way you want, but remember, heavy items go in the middle. Tie everything snug and tight. Don't want anything moving around going over rapids," ST says. "We'll be leaving soon, so take down your tent, sleeping bag and clothes and put them in watertight bags. Pack and tie them around the Igloo. After you have paid me back, we'll get you two of everything. One set to live here, and one set for the river."

ROJ gets everything assembled in his canoe. ST pulls on the supplies and says, "Well done. Tight as a drum. You learn fast, ROJ. You comfortable paddling in the stern for our trip?"

"No problem. I want to learn everything you have to teach me." "Great attitude. Especially since I have scheduled the next river trip in one week, and you will be guiding it. It's a small group of three or four on a short three to five days getting out at Santa Elena River Access. It's the same place I landed with you, if you remember," ST says.

"Don't remember any of that. All I remember is being catapulted ten feet in the air and landing up against a boulder. It was that boulder that saved my life," ROJ replies.

CHAPTER SEVENTEEN

ROJ, your first river trip will be arriving first thing tomorrow morning at the canoe launching site. There will be three or four in the group, so tie up two more canoes behind you and take them with you. If you are alone in a canoe by yourself, place the supplies in the bow to give you stability in the rapids. Call Rachael when you make it to the take-out at Santa Elena River Access, and someone will come pick up all of you. Make all the preparations the way you were shown. Since we work together as a family, you are in charge, and you get to delegate who does what to help you. Now do you have any questions before you begin the preparations?" ST asks.

"No. I pretty much have everything in hand. I'll begin making my list of supplies, then round up everyone to delegate the assignments. Can't wait to get started on my own. I've really been waiting for this. Thanks for this opportunity," ROJ replies.

"Hey, you earned it, and you have proven to me that you are tough and smart enough to handle yourself. Just be safe, and use your best calculating judgment with each and every rapid. Remember, if you don't treat each and every rapid with respect, it will bite you in the ass," ST scolds.

"Got it. I'll get started with my list and making meals for each day. See you later when I have everything ready to go." With preparations completed and the canoes loaded, it has taken nearly all day for ROJ to get everything ready for one river trip. He now knows how important family is when they all work together—something he has never experienced before. They may be a bunch of oddballs, but when it comes to what they all do best and live for—river trips—family is first and foremost. It is an experience that ROJ is starting to appreciate.

"Hey, FAM, what time is breakfast in the morning? I need to leave before eight," ROJ asks.

"Whenever I feel like it, dumb shit. I make breakfast when I get up." "Hey, I have a trip tomorrow, and I need my energy before leaving!" ROJ yells.

"Kidding, ass swipe. I'll have breakfast ready for you when you wake up," FAM replies rudely.

"Thank, FAM. You're the best," ROJ says, trying to kiss ass.

After waking up at 6:00 a.m., ROJ walks over to the fire where FAM really does have breakfast ready. A hearty helping of scrambled eggs, bacon, biscuits, and homemade gravy, and coffee. This is the breakfast he was force-fed back in his former life, but somehow, it tastes great the way FAM makes it. Trying to avoid any further insults to pile on from yesterday, ROJ simply nods in acceptance of the wonderful meal setting in front of him. Gorging himself and drinking three cups of coffee, he walks over to where FAM is sitting. He picks her up, stands her on her feet, and gives her a huge hug. Without saying a word, ROJ walks away back toward his tent. Just slightly, he looks over his shoulder. FAM is still standing there, staring at him motionless like a statue. He is very pleased with himself for giving FAM something she probably has not experienced before—a token of his love and appreciation.

Gathering the last of his supplies from his tent, ROJ heads down to the river where the canoes are beached, loaded up for a river trip. Everyone else is still sleeping except FAM, who is attending the fire. Glancing over toward her, she give ROJ a simple wave goodbye. He returns the wave while staring at her for a few seconds. She doesn't take her eyes off him until he pushes the tied-up canoes out into the river and starts paddling in the distance downstream.

ROJ arrives at the canoe launch site in town, rounds up his canoes, beaches them, and waits for his party. It's not long before a group of four approaches him. They are all young, in the mid- to late twenties, and the leader is the first to speak up, "Hello, my name is Weyland Reddington. Are you our guide?"

"Yes. My name is ROJ." ROJ shook Weyland's hand. "After I get your canoes loaded on the trailer, we will shuttle up to Redford where we will put in for your trip. If you will please bring your suitcases to the shuttle, you need to unpack them and repack your belongings in the watertight bags I have provided for you. You can then try on the life jackets to make sure they fit. You will be wearing them during the entire trip, so make sure they are comfortable and snug."

Weyland is tall, but not quite as tall as ROJ. He has well- groomed dark hair and presents himself with confidence. ROJ speculates that he must be the manager or supervisor of those people with him. He is also the only one who is properly dressed for a river trip. His attire consists of a flannel shirt, hat, sunglasses, loose painter's pants, and boots.

After they finish packing their belongings in the shuttle and have tried on their life jackets, Weyland makes the introductions. "ROJ, I would like you to meet the rest of my group. The guy in the tie-dyed T-shirt is Roger, the blond is Marcus, and this striking young woman is Sierra."

Roger is a reformed hippie out of college when he decided his cultural attire was finally out of place. Being from San Francisco, a lot of his father's friends were reformed hippies. He loved the irresponsible lifestyle it projected, but decided enough was enough. Marcus is from Philadelphia, stands 5' 8", and his blond hair is dyed. He always seems to have brown roots showing. He and Weyland met during a National Frisbee-Golf competition in his home town and hit it off right away. The lush of the group, Sierra, is as beautiful as they come. Don't let her good looks fool you. She is as sharp as a tack with a background in International Communications and Business Management. She fills out her 5' 7" frame in all the right places and has long flowing red hair. She doesn't flaunt her attractiveness but is very grounded in her beliefs and values. Living in a rural farming community in the Midwest allowed her to experience first hand the value of hard work. "I am glad to meet you all. When we reach Redford and get the canoes unloaded, I want to explain the type of canoes you will be using, the name of the different parts of

Michael E. Oppitz

106

the canoes, how to paddle, and how to walk through them without capsizing. First of all, do any of you have experience with canoes?" ROJ asks.

They all shake their heads no.

"OK, then. I will know what to expect from each of you." They board the shuttle and arrive in Redford shortly after.

ROJ announces instructions to untie the canoes and take them down to the beach where they can place their watertight bags. He secures all the bags, then begins with explaining the parts of the canoes.

"First of all, these canoes are seventeen-foot ABS plastic Tejas canoes. Virtually indestructible. Watch me as I show you how to walk through a canoe so you can repeat it every time. After a few tries, you'll be pros at it," ROJ says. He demonstrates how it's done and asks, "Who among you are the two strongest?"

Weyland is the first to raise his hand followed by Sierra. "All right, the other two will be in the bow, or the front, and you two will be in the stern, or the back. The sides are called the gun walls, and the support rods are the thwarts. Before we can launch, push the canoes partly in the river so Marcus and Roger can walk toward the bow seats," ROJ says.

With Roger and Marcus in position, ROJ checks the watertight bags once again. Weyland and Sierra get in their stern seats while ROJ gets in his. "When I say push off, Weyland and Sierra, slightly push off just a few feet so I can go over the paddling instructions," ROJ instructs them.

Once they are in position, ROJ says, "The bow rowers paddle from front to back right along the gun walls. You paddle on the sides instructed by the stern rowers. When paddling against the current in a certain direction, Roger and Marcus, you reach out perpendicular to the canoe and pull in with all your might. This is called reaching, something you will be doing a lot once we hit the rapids. You keep doing that until you get to where you want to be. Weyland and Sierra, you can back paddle on the side you want to turn and also it helps stabilize the canoe in rapids. In slack water, alternating the sides you both paddle will keep you going straight without losing speed. You decide the side you both paddle and yell the instructions. The Colorado Canyon is a leisurely trip with many small and enjoyable rapids. It will give you all plenty of time to get used to paddling and working together. If there are no questions, follow me," ROJ says.

As they take off, the occupants of each canoe takes time trying out their abilities in order to hone their skills. ROJ notices that Weyland and Sierra really are capable of giving out instructions, and they're not afraid to voice it. Their detail- oriented nature shows. ROJ gets closer to them and says, "While you are working things out, you should look at the beautiful volcanic sides of the canyon when we reach them very soon." Without notice, Marcus, who is with Sierra, shows his sign of protest toward her constant instructions by splashing her. In no time, she starts splashing him. Weyland and Roger begin in. While they start actually enjoying themselves, ROJ keeps his distance. He is reminded that this is their trip, not his. Their playful behavior continues on for a couple of hours when Sierra says, "ROJ, what is that roaring sound?" "That's your first set of rapids. They will all announce themselves with that sound. For each rapid we encounter, the water will form a V. That is called the notch, and it represents the entrance to the rapids. Look for it every time. Going through it is called 'shooting the notch.' As you go through the first set of rapids, back paddle, all of you, to slow your speed and keep your canoes stabilized. When you feel comfortable with your abilities, you can paddle forward to increase your speed on the upcoming rapids. But this first time, take it slow. Be careful, and find out how to work together," ROJ exclaims. "As we get closer, line up single file and follow me, doing everything I do."

Within twenty yards from the first rapid, ROJ looks over his shoulder to find that they listened to him and are in single file. Shooting the notch straight on, the first rapid is a straight shot through, and the two other canoes are back paddling just like instructed. Everyone is yelling and hollering shouts of joy except for Sierra. She is a lot more reserved, and ROJ could tell she, being the calculated one, is a tad nervous. Spilling out of the first rapid, the group gets together and are boasting their success. Sierra finally loosens up and starts splashing Weyland. ROJ paddles ahead while the others are enjoying themselves and getting wet. When they get all that out of their system, ROJ pulls up to them and announces that there is a tinaja up ahead where they can relax and swim in a natural spring-fed pool. Several more rapids are traversed just fine as the group learns quickly and paddles through with more confidence than ROJ could have anticipated.

"If you will follow me to the tinaja up ahead, I'll get lunch ready. There's lots to see, so take a little time to walk around and swim."

"I don't know about the rest of you, but I'm going swimming," Sierra announces. After beaching the canoes, Sierra rights herself, stretches her arms over her head, then falls back to a relaxed position. She begins with grabbing her t-shirt by the bottom and pulling it slowly over her head. Her low rise shorts give evidence of a pierced belly button, and her natural physique exposes her beautiful torso and ribs. Next, she unbuttons her shorts. Pulling down her zipper gives light to her beautiful curves. All the while, she has a captive audience. Her long red hair is so striking anything looks good on her. Her bright-pink swimsuit captures the attention of Marcus and Roger. They just stare as she runs over to the tinaja and jumps right in. "*Eowww*, the water's cold but feels great. Who wants to join me?"

Marcus wastes no time and bravely walks over to the pool. "Come on, scaredy cat. The best way to get in is to just jump in," Sierra says.

"Look out, here I come," Marcus yells. One jump, and he yells even louder that Sierra did. "I didn't believe you, but I do now. Never experienced anything like this before. This is definitely something to write home about."

While Weyland and Roger walk around exploring, ROJ gets lunch ready consisting of deli sandwiches, potatoes salad, veggies and dip, and soda and water. After thirty minutes, they all walk in minutes apart from one another. The first meal of the day allows them all to totally relax and reflect on the day so far.

"I had no idea that canoeing could be such a rush," Weyland says kind out of character. His relaxed demeanor and honesty takes everyone by surprise, and they are struck by silence until Sierra speaks up, "Weyland, I didn't know you knew what a rush actually felt like unless you smoked weed in your youth."

"My dear Sierra, there are a lot of things you don't know about me, rushes and all. I haven't felt this relaxed and close to nature in a long time. I just hope that I can take my reflections of this trip and apply them to my personal and professional life and be a better person for it," Weyland says with a soft honesty in his voice. No one says another thing except nodding in agreement. "What do you say we chow down on this perfect lunch ROJ has assembled for us?"

They devour lunch with laughter and talking, and ROJ looks on with a big smile on his face.

"So, ROJ, what's next for us downriver?" Marcus speaks up. "There are quite a few more small rapids before leaving the Colorado. Depending on how much time we have left when that happens depends on whether or not we can tackle some of the class II and III rapids going into Santa Elena. You'll want to have something to eat and keep up your strength before entering the class IIs and IIIs. While you all get your canoes ready, I'll pack up lunch so we can get underway," ROJ says.

CHAPTER EIGHTEEN

A s they launch their canoes and head downstream, Sierra and Marcus take the lead. ROJ notices that Sierra's tentative attitude has been replaced with confidence and fearlessness. ROJ pulls up beside her and says, "You don't appear to be the tentative schoolgirl I first met this morning. I'm glad to see that, Sierra. You'll need every ounce of your newly found energy when we encounter the class IIs."

Sierra just nods in agreement and continues paddling, and a huge smile appears on her face. The group traverses three more rapids, and there's only forty-five minutes left before the sun disappears behind the canyon walls. "ROJ, when do we get out of the Colorado Canyon?" Weyland shouts above the last rapids.

"Tomorrow afternoon will be your last rapid in the Colorado. I suggest we find a flat area where we can beach our canoes."

ROJ pulls ahead of everyone and finds a suitable beach area. "Pull up there and set up camp. I'll show you how to construct your tents."

Michael E. Oppitz

As soon as the canoes are beached, ROJ says, "Who wants to be first to set up your tent?"

"I'm not bashful or ashamed. I'll go first," Sierra says. She digs out her tent, and she and ROJ walk to a level area. "I want all you to follow us so you'll know how to set up yours." Within five minutes, ROJ has Sierra's tent set up. "Five minutes to you, ROJ, is like thirty to us," Roger complains. ROJ just walks away and says, "You can help each other.

That's what teamwork is all about."

ROJ is busy getting the fire started and preparing supper. He has several pots of water sitting on the grill with bags of beef stroganoff, spaghetti with meatballs, green beans, corn, and brats. Weyland walks up to him and asks, "How many days will we be on the river, ROJ?"

"All day tomorrow and the next day. Depending on how long it takes us to go through the class II and III rapids before the river access will determine how soon you all can put in on the third day. We won't know that until we reach those class II rapids," ROJ replies.

"Are class II rapids difficult?" After hearing that question from Weyland, Roger makes his way over to the fire.

"The water level can change any day. One day can be completely different than the next. If you all learn as much as possible and are comfortable working together, those rapids should not be difficult. A very important thing you can communicate with your group is to listen and follow instructions. That will determine how well you and your friends navigate rapids," ROJ says.

Roger interjects by saying, "How are class II rapids different from the small one we have been going through?"

"Class II has obstacles, more current, switchbacks, and sometimes, multiple notches to shoot through. That's why it's important to learn how to communicate with your partner and work together," ROJ says.

"Will you please go through this with everyone in the morning before we shove off?" Weyland asks.

"Sure. I'll be glad to. Supper will be ready in about ten. Round up everyone, and I'll break out the wine," ROJ says. While they are eating and drinking and having a great time talking about their day, ROJ hears Weyland talking about a problem identified with one of their employees. He does not mean to eavesdrop on any of their conversations, but for some reason, his attention is drawn toward it. ROJ comes to find out that a new employee that was recommended by another employee was accused of stealing an insignificant item from the stocking room by the line supervisor. There was a lot of discussion about what procedure to use and whether or not just a reprimand would be enough.

"Weyland, please excuse me for intruding. With you permission, can ask you a question?" ROJ asks.

"Sure, ROJ. Shoot."

"This employee you are talking about, how well do you know him?"

ROJ inquires.

"Never actually met him. He works on the production line, and I get information about him and his actions through the line supervisor," Weyland replies.

"How well does your line supervisor know him?"

"What are you getting at, ROJ?" Weyland says, kind of annoyed. "All I'm saying, sir, is that you are reacting to information derived from one individual."

"Yeah, my line supervisor. That's his job," Weyland retorts. "It's obvious this employee did something to demand reprimanding circumstances toward his actions, and I was wondering how well your line supervisor has communicated this employee's motivation toward his actions—whether or not he was encouraged to do what he did, or whether he felt compelled," ROJ replies.

"I don't really know where you are going with this, ROJ, but I think you are butting into business that's not yours," Weyland says, irritated.

"May I reflect with you what the Bible says in John chapter 8 when onlookers wanted to stone Mary for being caught red- handed for adultery? When Jesus asked the witnesses to cast the first stone who were without sin, there was no one left to accuse her. All I'm saying is for you to make a simple effort on your own to find out what happened, allow this employee to acknowledge his wrongdoing and take responsibility for his actions. If you are satisfied with his response and you personally offer him another chance to redeem himself, I think you'll find that this employee could possibly turn out to be one of your best and most trusted employees in your company. Just food for thought, that's all," ROJ says.

Weyland just sits there, frozen in silence. The rest of his group don't know what to say either. It's possible to surmise that these people of great importance and stature have never come across anything like this before. It appears to be a concept foreign to them.

Finally, Marcus break the silence by saying, "Weyland, if something like this actually works, you'll have to write about it and establish new policies, and maybe even follow Lester Jones, making a case study about it."

"Unbelievable. How did you come up with something like that, ROJ?" Weyland asks.

"It just seems straightforward to me, being in misunderstood situations before," ROJ responds.

"Don't worry, son. I'll give Lester Jones the chance you suggested and hope that he does turn around. He may never know what kind of angel he has looking out for him, but I do," Weyland says, looking ROJ straight in the eyes. "I do." They continue eating, drinking, and enjoying one another's company. "I have to tell you, ROJ, I have never eaten such delicious food before, heated up from a bag. If I didn't know any better, I would consider this gourmet food in comparison to what I can order from any restaurant," Weyland exclaims. "I'll second that," Roger says. "I know everything tastes better cooked outdoors, but this is truly some of the best I have eaten in a long time. You are a master, ROJ."

"Thank you for your kind words. There's more where this came from, so I hope you like the rest of the meals I have prepared for you."

"By the way, what time is it?" Roger asks.

"Why? Is there some place you have to be?" Sierra quips. "I was just asking because it seems to be getting dark faster than normal," Roger says. "Is there a reason why, ROJ, there is not as much sunlight?"

"If you look around you, what do you see?" ROJ asks. "Oh yeah. There are canyons. Kind of like living in the mountains. The sun goes down behind them sooner than normal."

"I would suggest an early evening since you will be busy tomorrow with class II rapids. You'll be using muscles you probably haven't used before, so you will all need a good night's sleep. I'll wake you in the morning with a hearty breakfast," ROJ announces.

ROJ cleans up after supper and gets everything put away. He leaves out a one-gallon jug of wine for the group to finish off. As he climbs in his tent, he can still hear them talking and laughing. He smiles because he knows they will find out the hard way the advice he tried to share with them. Anyway, ROJ keeps reminding himself that this is their trip and probably a once-in-a-lifetime trip for them all. It's not long before he falls asleep.

CHAPTER NINETEEN

T he next morning, ROJ's internal biological clock wakes him up at 5:00 a.m. He climbs out of his tent, greeted with a light fog. He knows it won't last long since the rising sun will burn it off quickly. It's just that everything is wet, a rude awakening for the group. ROJ finds dry driftwood in the bottom of a pile and begins making a fire for breakfast. Coffee is the first thing he works on. In no time, the smell begins to permeate the other tents. As he unpacks the kitchen supplies to start breakfast, Weyland is the first to emerge.

"I thought I smelled coffee. Smells so much better when made outdoors."

"I think you'll find everything tastes better when made outdoors," ROJ replies.

With fire roaring and the skillets hot, the crackling sound and smell of bacon wakes up everyone else. "What the hell is the time?" Sierra complains as she rolls out of her tent.

Michael E. Oppitz

"You don't want to know," Marcus quickly answers. "Just get your butt over here and get some of this delicious food." "Wow," Sierra says as she tastes the scrambled eggs cooked in butter and bacon slathered on top of biscuits and gravy. "I never thought something so simple could taste so delicious. You are going to spoil us all the longer we stay with you, ROJ." "That's the plan. I aim to make this trip the most memorable in every way I can, and starting with your stomachs is always a good place to begin," ROJ says, chuckling.

"Well, you have already mastered that. What's on the schedule for today?" Weyland asks.

"As soon as we leave here, there is another one half day of easy paddling and small rapids before leaving the Colorado. Before that happens, there are two chutes to tackle. They are a lot of fun, and I think you'll all love it. Then, the real fun begins," ROJ says.

"What do you mean by the real fun begins?" quips Roger.

"You'll meet your first class II and III rapids right after lunch. At that time, I'll go over with you what to expect and exactly how to run them. This is very important. You must do exactly as I tell you, and no messing around unless any of you want to go for a swim and chasing your supplies downstream," ROJ says sternly.

"No problem, ROJ. Just tell us what to do when we get there," Weyland answers for everyone.

"OK, pack up your tents and personal stuff. When I'm done packing up the kitchen supplies, we'll be ready to launch. You have thirty minutes," ROJ says.

119

Everyone is busy packing up their clothes and sleeping bags, then rolling up the tents. ROJ inspects each canoe to make sure it is packed and tied correctly. After loading up everything in the bow of his canoe, they push off. The fog burns off soon after they are on the river. "We're in no rush, so just enjoy yourselves. The chutes are not far from here."

When they start getting close to the chutes, Sierra notices a bunch of canoes lined up waiting for something. "ROJ, what's that up ahead? Why are those canoes lined up like that?"

"We are about to enter the chutes The water is channeled in between two chutes so your speed will really pick up as you go through them. Don't worry. It's fun, and don't try to paddle. You'll just make it worse if you try," ROJ says.

"What do you mean, don't paddle?" Sierra shouts. "There's no room for you to put your oar in the water.

Just enjoy the experience, and watch everyone in front of you on how they do it. You'll have fun. I promise," ROJ says enduringly.

The line of canoes dwindles, and the group can now see what's going on. The expressions on their faces turn from apprehension to excitement. "Let me in there," Roger says right away. "I want to go first!"

Weyland gets them in position, and surprisingly, the current of water going through the first chute pulls them through like water going down a drain. Weyland keeps his oar close to his chest while Roger waves his oar above his head like a crazy kid. He's hooping and hollering.

Sierra is watching them in amazement. "I can do this. It's supposed to be fun. OK, Marcus, here we go." Their canoe is suddenly pulled into the rapid current going through the chute. They can't believe the rush they are feeling. Just before they exit, Marcus raises his oar above his head, and Sierra follows suit.

As they join the others, ROJ lets them laugh about their newfound experience. "Hey, is that another one up ahead?" Roger shouts.

"You have good eyes, Roger," ROJ says. "Have at it."

As they paddle their way to the other chute, they are amazed how many people there are. Families playing along the beach having picnics, kids running and splashing everywhere, and young people their age swimming and playing. "This place is totally popular," Marcus responds in amazement.

"There are a lot of people who canoe to this place just to spend the day. It is extremely popular for those who camp in Big Bend a lot," ROJ says.

As they near the second chute, Sierra says, "I want to go first this time. It's about time I did something first on this trip." She and Marcus line up their canoe straight on toward the chute, and as before, the current sucks them in.

This time, Sierra and Marcus both are waving their oars above their heads screaming and shouting like little kids. Weyland just shakes his head in approval. "People I work with and respect have turned into little kids," Weyland says, looking at ROJ.

"Is that a good thing?" ROJ responds with a big smile on his face.

"That's a very good thing, and I hope it happens more often. Did you know, ROJ, that the most successful people in the world have something very much in common with children?"

"No, what's that, Weyland?"

"They know how to get back up when they fall or are beaten down. They just don't give up, and that's what little kids do. They don't know how to fail. They just get back up."

"Have you shared that with them?" ROJ asks.

"I think it's time that I do because now they will have a reference of how it works," Weyland replies.

ROJ nods his head in approval while Weyland continues smiling and watching his friends have the time of their lives.

Weyland and Roger shoot the last chute, and they too are waving their oars above their heads shouting and laughing.

"I guess leaders can be kids too," ROJ says to himself.

As they continue paddling away from the chutes, Marcus is looking around and up at the canyons. "Are the canyon walls getting taller?"

"Very observant, Marcus. Yes, we are starting to enter the Santa Elena Canyon," ROJ says.

"When you hear the volume of the roar change, you'll know we are close to the class II rapids," ROJ says.

"That's not really a comforting thought," Sierra replies.

Traversing three small rapids easily seems to give everyone a lot of confidence. A half mile later, the canyon walls begin to change. They become higher, and the river becomes more narrow. Their pace picks up. ROJ sees a

Michael E. Oppitz

small beach on the left before entering the canyon. "OK, everyone, hit that beach on the left, and I'll get lunch ready. You'll have a little time to walk around and explore, but don't be gone too long," ROJ says.

When the canoes are beached and everyone is walking around stretching their legs, ROJ gets lunch ready, made of finger food, sandwiches, containers of potato salad and coleslaw, cheeses, and veggies with dip. It's not long before the group is scarfing down the spread ROJ has assembled. "You all act as if you haven't eaten for a week." ROJ. Chuckles. "We haven't worked this hard for a long time, and our appetites have really increased with the gobs of delicious food you always have ready for us. Just can't get enough," Weyland says.

"I'll take that as a compliment," ROJ says.

CHAPTER TWENTY

While they are stuffing their faces, ROJ goes over the plan for the first class II rapids they are about to encounter. "When the current begins to pick up, look for the notch on the right, and follow me through it. As soon as you do, bow people, reach as hard as you can to the left, and don't stop reaching until you make it to the big boulder clear on the left. There's an eddy where we will assemble. Once you all make it there, I will go over plan B. Remember, reach hard and don't stop. Stern people, row hard as you can on your right, maintaining the speed you need and keeping your canoe parallel with the current. Any questions so far?"

"What happens if we don't make it to the boulder on the left?" Sierra hesitantly asks.

There was no answer from ROJ. "You have ten more minutes to relax and eat, then I'm cleaning up so we can push off. Remember, keep your game face on until we get through this first rapid, then you can relax."

ROJ cleans up lunch, repacks the leftovers, and notices that everyone is in their canoes ready to push off. "Let's go. Remember, when entering the first notch of the rapid, keep in single file, and watch what I do."

There isn't much chattering from the group because they seem intent and somewhat unreserved as to what they are going to be facing for the first time in their lives.

"The current is picking up, ROJ. Does that mean we are getting closer?" Sierra shouts above the roar of the oncoming rapids.

"Good observation, Sierra All right, you know what to do. Just watch what I do and paddle hard Don't stop until you reach the boulder on the left Here we go!" ROJ yells.

ROJ enters the notch and immediately paddles hard on the right side, maintaining speed and keeping parallel with the current Within twenty seconds, he's over on the left side of the river, safely located in the eddy of the big boulder He waves for the next canoe to enter. Weyland stops back paddling and enters the notch. He immediately begins paddling hard on his right and yells to Roger to keep reaching on his left. "Come on, Roger, you piece of shit. Get us over there. I'm not going swimming because of you!"

Roger paddles like a machine, and to their surprise, their canoe is responding to their will. It's heading straight to where ROJ is sitting behind the boulder. "Hey, you made it. Good job guys."

"What do you mean I'm a piece of shit?" Roger retorts. "It just came out during the spur of the moment. I apologize, Roger. I really didn't meant it," Weyland says.

Just then, Sierra and Marcus enter the notch. Marcus is reaching left, but not as hard as he should. Sierra is frightened, and it shows on her face. She's trying to paddle as hard as she can, but they are not moving. They're just holding their own waiting for something bad to happen when they run out of gas and become fatigued. "Excuse me, fellows, got to get out there," ROJ calmly says. With a big back paddle, he turns his canoe into the current. Fighting with everything he has by paddling on his left, he reaches Sierra's canoe. ROJ back paddles one more time, turning his canoe on a dime and winds up on their right side. He starts paddling hard on his right instructing Sierra to do the same. With ROJ's help, they both start moving in the direction of the boulder, still remaining parallel to the current but staying away from the rocks.

As their canoe gets close to the boulder, Roger reaches out and grabs hold of Sierra's canoe, pulling it in to safety within the eddy of the boulder. ROJ circles around them all and gets in the eddy. "Well, kids, have you had enough fun, yet?" ROJ says jokingly.

"What we just did was no joking matter. I got stuck out there and didn't know what to do, and that was just our first rapid," Sierra shouts in frustration.

"No, Sierra, that was just one half of the rapid. You still have to go through the rest of it," ROJ replies.

Sierra bows and shakes her head. A moment later, she says, "Give me a minute, and I'll be ready."

"OK, ROJ, now what?" Weyland asks.

"The reason we are here is because I didn't think you were capable of changing direction in the middle of the current, dodging rocks at the same in order to find the next notch. If you look closely, you now have to go back into the current, paddle hard enough to stay away from those rocks jetting one third out in the river, then hit the next notch created by that other big boulder in the middle. Go through the first notch you come to. If you try to go around the boulder, you could get caught up against it, watching you canoe disappear under the current with all your belongs. Once again, watch me and do exactly as I do. No exemptions. Any questions?" ROJ explains.

All their eyes are fixed on ROJ as he explains what needs to be done. Tunnel vision has set in as they absorb everything he just said. "No exemptions," Sierra says under her breath.

Weyland heard what she said, and he gives her an encouraging nod. He replies under his breath as well, "You can do it."

ROJ back paddles allowing his canoe to catch the current. He then paddles hard on the left side, keeping him parallel with the current, getting him past the rock wall. Just as he reaches the big boulder in the middle of the river, he back paddles on the left, turning him on a dime and shooting him through the notch in seconds. He then back paddles hard on the right, turning him on a dime once again and into the eddy of that boulder where he waits and watches the group. "OK, who's next?" ROJ shouts over the roar of the rapids.

Sierra is shaking her head no just as Weyland back paddles and is thrust into the current. While he paddles hard on the left, he yells at Roger to paddle harder. Their efforts work, and they make it past the rock wall. Just as they reach the boulder, ROJ yells, "Now," and Weyland back paddles, turning his canoe into the notch. "Hit it again on the right," ROJ shouts again, and their canoe joins ROJ in the eddy behind the boulder.

ROJ waves to Sierra. It's obvious she's scared, and it shows on her expression. She looks away from them all, and bows her head and begins to sob. Marcus doesn't know what to do or say. A moment later, her sobbing stops. As Sierra contemplates what to do and try to save face at the same time, her courage slowly begins to emanate throughout her body. With adrenaline beginning to pulsate through her veins, the hair on her arms stand up straight, and a chill gives her a shiver. She realizes this is her wakeup call. Just then, she changes her scared expression to that of fighter pilot. There is suddenly a look of determination on her face, and she is screaming something to Marcus that can't be heard over the roar of the rapid. "Marcus, you are going to paddle your brains out and help us get over there or I'm going to pound you to dust! Do you get my drift?"

Marcus doesn't say a thing. He just nods. "Here we go. Get ready!" Sierra shouts. She back paddles sending them into the current. Marcus paddles so hard, he's not sure whether he's more afraid of the current or what Sierra will do to him if he doesn't pull through. They are both paddling hard on the left moving them in the direction of the boulder. Sierra is paddling with more determination than anyone has ever seen. Their canoe finally reaches the boulder just a few feet from total disaster. ROJ yells at the top of his lungs, "Now, Sierra. Now!" She back paddles on the left shooting them through the notch. Then ROJ says to her again, "Now. Right now!" Sierra back paddles once again, but on the right, turning them into the safety of the eddy.

As soon as the eddy catches and holds them, she bows her head and starts crying. No one says a thing for what seems like several minutes. "Can we go now?" Sierra says.

"Go where?" Weyland asks. "Anywhere but here."

"When we leave this eddy and finish going through the rest of the rapids, which is easy, let's beach on the left so you all can rest for a bit," ROJ says. "Follow me. It's easy from here."

They all back paddle one at a time following ROJ through the remaining rapids and wind up on the beach to the left.

Sierra gets out of her canoe, walks off her frustration and returns to the group. "Sierra, compared to what you do an a daily basis calculating risks, formulating step-by- step procedures and being responsible for the decisions you make, how would you use the accomplishments, emotions, and decisions you just made to avoid certain disaster but wound up being successful for a team effort?" Weyland asks point-blank.

Sierra is dumbstruck by Weyland's question and is taken back by what kind of answer she can possibly give. Not necessarily looking at him but looking in his direction, she says, "I did something just now that I never thought I was capable of doing. I didn't do it alone, either. I had all of you to help me and encourage me. Through mere frustration and determination, I found the courage and willpower to make it happen. Even though I love what I do back in the world and I do it very well, this encounter proved to me that there's always other ways of doing something differently and, well, and one can never be so proud as not to ask for assistance to help guide my thoughts and decisions."

"Couldn't have said it better myself. Congratulations," Weyland says, giving her a small hug.

"I can see now why you are the boss, Weyland. It takes a gifted individual like yourself to think outside the box and bring us all on a journey like this one to give us different insights and perspectives not only about ourselves, but about life and its challenges. I don't think I could have thought about something like that," Sierra says.

Roger and Marcus don't reply but just nod their heads in approval. "Just from observation alone, I can tell you all have learned some new things about yourselves and each other," ROJ interjects.

"ROJ, you are truly an amazing guide, and I thank you for keeping us safe while making this trip fun and about us. When we make it to our take-out safely and get home, I will definitely recommend you to everyone I know," Weyland says. "Thank you, sir. Kind words like that are always appreciated."

"What's next, ROJ?" Weyland asks.

"Since we are stuck in these canyons and can't get out until we reach our take-out destination at the river access, I suggest making camp here before we lose the sun behind these canyon walls. You can all regroup and push hard in order to make it to the access by afternoon tomorrow or the next morning," ROJ explains.

"What kind of rapids are ahead of us?" Marcus asks. "I'll go over that with you tomorrow after breakfast. You all need some rest. I'll get a fire started for supper."

ROJ gets out another gallon of wine, and everyone is content just sitting around a big, warming fire drinking wine and laughing. ROJ surprises them by throwing on five sirloin steaks that instantly crackle on the hot grill. "ROJ, you really aim to spoil us. I would never think that I would be treated to grilled steaks out in the middle of nowhere and drinking wine at the same time. You truly are a gifted guide, and spoiling us rotten," Weyland says.

"That's why I love what I do. It's very pleasing to me to see you all enjoying yourselves, and spoiling you is all part of the experience."

"Well, I know one thing," Roger adds. "I'm going to have to let out my belt by making another hole. I can tell I have gained weight while working hard at the same time."

During the rest of supper, there is just light chatter. After everyone finishes eating, it's not long before they are all in their tents, sawing logs.

CHAPTER TWENTY-ONE

Morning comes early as ROJ rejuvenates the old coals and has a roaring fire going with fresh coffee. Weyland is the first to emerge from his tent. "That's one smell I will really miss. You have really spoiled us, ROJ, with your attention to detail and keeping us fed like kings and queens. You should really be proud of what you do. It shows in everything you do."

ROJ returns his compliment with an approving nod. Roger is the next to wake up. While trying to walk through the zipper door, he stumbles and falls head over heels. "Who is that? Is that you, Roger?" Sierra shouts from her sleeping bag. "Who else do you know who can make something hard out of something easy?" Roger shouts in return. "Get your butt out of bed and have some coffee with me."

A minute later, Sierra joins the partial group at the fire where ROJ is preparing his usual awesome breakfast. The smell of eggs finally gets Marcus out of his tent. "I know of some eggs that have my name on them."

"Well, hurry up, then. I'm starting at the S of your name and working backward!" Sierra shouts.

Marcus shoots through the tent flap and makes a beeline to the fire. While they are enjoying breakfast and stuffing their faces, they finally look up at one another and start laughing. Weyland's hair is sticking straight up, Roger's hair is all pushed to one side, Sierra's hair looks like a huge bird's nest, and Marcus's hair looks like it was hit with electricity. "If we took a picture of ourselves, either no one would believe it, or it would go viral on social media," Sierra says.

"I'm scared to know what could happen. I think whatever happens on the river stays on the river," Roger says.

"Good advice, Roger. I agree," Weyland replies. "What do you have planned for us today, ROJ?"

"There are a few more rapids, class II and a III. The biggest one of them all is called the Rock Slide, where fast water is channeled around a house-sized boulder. But the rapid is straight, just fast. Then a couple of canyons where you can get out and explore. After that, you'll be at your take-out. If you push hard, you can be out before nightfall, or you can camp out one more night and get out the next day. It's entirely up to you," ROJ says.

"We'll see how it goes with time. What are we to expect with the next rapids?" Marcus interjects.

"The next class II is pretty much straight through. No switchbacks or cutting across the current. Just follow me straight through. Remember to back paddle in order to control your speed going through. The class III after that has a huge boulder in the middle of the river, but it is relatively easy to shoot the notch on either side. We'll reconvene after that."

While they finish breakfast, their laughter continues. The sky is getting lighter as the sun tries to creep over the canyon walls. The chill in the air is lifting quickly as the group begins shedding jackets and sweaters. Bird songs can be heard everywhere, and the bats are seen flying to their nests and crevices in the tall canyon walls. There's a sense of exhilaration in the air as everyone is excited for another day on the river. As the last person finishes up breakfast, ROJ is busy packing up his kitchen supplies while the group rummages through their tents, stuffing their watertight bags. The tents come down and are packed in the canoes.

"OK, everyone, five minutes, and we shove off," ROJ announces. As they finally push off from shore, ROJ says, "The next rapid is just ahead, so follow me through." As ROJ shoots through the notch, Sierra, who is in the third canoe, sees him gliding through the rapids with no problem. She is astonished of his speed as his canoe bounces along the submerged rocks. She hopes she can do the same without capsizing.

Weyland and Roger shoot the notch and are gliding along with good speed and choose not to back paddle. As Sierra shoots through the notch, she immediately begins back paddling to slow her speed. ROJ, who is already through the rapid, is shouting something to her, but the roar of the rapids drowns out everything. Finally, Sierra senses she has control of the situation. Instead of back paddling, she suddenly starts paddling forward and shouts to Marcus to do the same. Their speed picks up so fast Marcus almost falls backward in his seat. "Wow, what a rush!" Sierra exclaims at the top of her voice. "Let's get it on!"

She can see the other two canoes waiting in slack water since they all made it through without any problems. Sierra can see a clear line of sight through the rapids and yells to Marcus once again. "Come on, let's get it on!" They are both paddling as hard as they can, and now they are canoeing faster than the flow of water, which is already traveling at five to six knots. ROJ's eyes get big since he has not seen anyone paddle through this rapid this fast before. He's just hoping they make it through safely.

As Sierra and Marcus get close, the other two canoes can hear Sierra yelling and hollering at the top of her lungs, "What a rush! Didn't know I had it in me. That really was awesome. Can't wait for the next one."

Weyland looks at ROJ and says, "I think I have created a monster."

Sierra and Marcus join the other canoes and start laughing with excitement.

"Sierra, I was very worried for you. I haven't seen you paddle that confidently since starting the trip. What got into you?" ROJ asks.

"I haven't the foggiest. The urge come over me so suddenly I just had to act. It just seemed like something I had to do or lose it. Have you ever felt like that before?"

"Yes, all the time when my parents were controlling every day of my life. There were many times when I just wanted to scream or do something foolish or act out to let my body know that I was still alive. I'm glad you found your aha moment. I hope you have more of them," ROJ replies. "I hope you all find your aha moments even though not everyone has one. Congratulations, Sierra. You were a lot of fun to watch."

Sierra giggles with ROJ's response. Weyland and Roger just shake their heads, but with big smiles on their faces.

"The next rapid, which is a class III and called the Rock Slide and not that difficult, is just ahead. You'll be hearing its roar in no time. There is a house-size boulder in the middle, and the notches on either side are fast. Make sure you are perfectly ready before shooting the notch. It's considered a class III for the water's speed and for what happens if you capsize. Follow me closely, and you all will be just fine," ROJ explains.

Paddling through flat water for a short while, the other canoes are busy with chatter. As ROJ looks in their direction, Sierra no longer has that look of serious concern on her face. Instead, it has been replaced with laughter and smiles. What a huge change she has gone through. A city girl who has been deathly afraid of doing anything dangerous or sporadic and has looked her fears straight in the eyes can find the sudden courage to tackle those fears and come out smiling and laughing. ROJ is thinking as he watches the group having the time of their lives, *I truly have found my calling and have the best job in the world. Can't see myself doing anything else. They deserve this experience, and I'm glad I can be a part of it.* The current picks up as the roar of the next rapid makes itself known. Actually, it sounds more like a *"roar in your face"* kind of sound. It's time for the group to get their game faces on again, and they have already established theirs. ROJ gets closer to the other canoes and shouts out instructions. "Remember, follow me through the notch because once you have committed yourselves, the current through this rapid is twice that of anything you have experienced so far. Back paddling will help, but more importantly, keep your paddles in the water at all times, steering. Watch me when I start paddling and on which side in order to point your canoes in the right direction. Keep a cool head, and you will be fine."

"ROJ, I think I'm scared for this one. I don't know if I can react that fast," Sierra says desperately.

"Sierra, you have already looked your fears in the eyes and come out smiling. Put your nervous energy into reaction energy and get mad. Get mad at this thing, and don't let it get away with anything. That will help sharpen your perspective and fine-tune your reaction time. If you feel doubtful in any way, remember, get mad. Don't let it get away with anything. Get mad and stay mad until you make it through," ROJ encourages her.

"OK, I'll try."

"No, you won't. You are not going to try. You are going to do it. No exceptions, remember? Do your understand me? You are going to do it! Now, start getting mad, and I want you right behind me. If I have the chance to turn around to look at you, you'd better be mad! Do you understand?" ROJ shouts at her.

"Yes, ROJ. I understand."

"All right then. Do as I do," ROJ instructs her. "Here we go."

As ROJ encounters the notch, the other two canoes are surprised at how fast the current swallows him through. Within a millisecond, he's paddling hard on his right to swing around the house size boulder. Then he switches sides and starts paddling on his left, swinging him around it. All of that happened within ten seconds. Sierra plunges through the notch. All of a sudden she's shouting out obscenities at Marcus to start reaching on his left as she paddles hard on her right. The whole time she's shouting out instructions. She's surprised how her commands are maneuvering her canoe just as she wants. Seconds later, she's shouting out instructions for Marcus to reach on his right as she paddles hard on her left, swinging the canoe around the other side. Just as she makes it around the huge boulder, she sees ROJ holding tight in the eddy of a smaller boulder with a big smile on his face, kind of like "I told you so." Without him having to say a word, a smile gradually appears on Sierra's face. She back paddles hard on the right, swinging her canoe into the eddy alongside ROJ.

"It's very nice to see you," ROJ says.

Sierra just nods her head, keeping the smile evident. Meanwhile, Weyland and Roger have already committed themselves through the notch. As Roger reaches on his left, Weyland is not paddling as hard as he should. He has not anticipated the speed of the current as well as he should have. Roger reaches repeatedly, but the canoe's stern bumps up against the house-size boulder. There's no room for Weyland to put his oar in the water. To his credit, Roger continues reaching. Weyland jabs at the boulder, trying to push them away, before the current capsizes their canoe and swallows them below the waterline. Weyland is able to move the canoe with just enough room to get his oar back in the water. He then shouts out instructions for Roger to start reaching on the right as Weyland paddles on the left, swinging the canoe around the boulder. All this time, the canoe is scraping along the sides of the boulder, barely giving Weyland room to paddle.

To their astonishment, they make it around the boulder, float downstream just far enough, and see the other two canoes holding up in the eddy on the right. With a hard back paddle on the right, Weyland swings their canoe alongside them.

"Whew! That was a close one. Guess I didn't respect the current as much as I should have. Must have been sheer determination that got us out of that predicament," Weyland says, wiping his forehead.

"I wouldn't say you were lucky even though you were, but you found a way to get it done. That is sheer determination," ROJ says. "No more rapids left, just a few narrow canyons to go through before your take- out. It's mostly flat water from here out, but the canyons will funnel the current in order to pick up your speed some. Look around you and enjoy all the sights and sounds. I think it's time for lunch, so you can all gather yourselves. There's no beach in these canyons, so we can have lunch here. Everyone tie off around this boulder, and I'll get some sandwiches and finger food."

ROJ gives Marcus his rope so he can tie off both canoes. ROJ gets out some sandwiches along with cheese, veggies, pickles, gorp, and marshmallows for dessert. This lunch situation is not like what they were expecting; nonetheless, everyone seems content and relaxed enjoying a simple lunch with good company. "Now, this is something worth writing home about," Sierra says, breaking the silence. Everyone simply nods their heads in approval while stuffing their faces. "You said we may be able to camp out tonight, extending our. "Yes, that's true. As we travel down through these canyons, there will be some places where you can get out and explore. But I have to tell you. Camping tonight will not be anything like it has been. There's no beach to get out and make a big fire or set up your tents. You'll be roughing it if you choose to spend the night in these canyons. And if you choose to get out and explore, nightfall will come early with these 1,500- foot canyon walls. You all must decide what you want to do."

As they all continue eating lunch, the expressions on their faces changes. Sierra speaks up and says, "I don't think I want to sleep in a canoe eating a cold supper. If I can't stop and eat in relaxation and sleep in a comfortable tent, I'm for pushing hard to make it to our take-out by nightfall."

"Don't want you want to do something worth writing home about?" Roger says.

"Already done that. I'm for getting out by tonight," Sierra replies. "Weyland, what about you?" Roger asks.

"I'll do whatever you all want to do. You don't need me to make decisions for you on the river," Weyland says.

"I guess the decision is up to you, Marcus. Any thoughts?" Sierra asks. "I'm for pushing hard and getting out by nightfall." "OK. It's all settled, then. After lunch, we will push hard through the canyons in order to make it to the river access before nightfall," ROJ says. "The next canyon is called Fern Canyon. It has a very unique surprise awaiting you."

When they all finish lunch, ROJ packs up the remaining containers and pushes off from the eddy. The current catches his canoe, pushing him easily downstream. The other two canoes follow suit. ROJ establishes the cadence while the others constantly row at the same speed. As they enter Fern Canyon, their pace quickens as the current is being squeezed. Sierra is the first to say something. "Hey, look at those canyon walls. The unconformity of the rock layers makes it look we are going backward. What a rush."

"Now, that is worth writing home about," Weyland says. "This optical illusion is really awesome. Never seen anything like it before."

"I think this a first for all of us. This is something special. Can't wait to try to explain this to my kids. They will never believe me," Marcus replies.

"You'll have to bring them all on this trip sometime," Sierra says. "Only if ROJ is my guide. Don't want anyone else. He's proven to be the best, and he definitely has earned my respect."

"I believe he has earned the respect from all of us, especially me. His insight has enlightened me to look at certain situations in a different light," Weyland says.

As they marvel at the illusion going through Fern Canyon, ROJ points out Smuggler's Cave up on the right on the Mexican side. "Many bandits and refugees have taken refuge in those caves. It's a nice hike up there, but I don't think we have time if you want to make the take- out on time."

"It's hard to believe that people actually lived in those caves," Sierra says.

"That type of living would be a welcome sight, if you are desperate enough," Weyland replies.

They all silently nod in approval as they float by. ROJ continues with the cadence. Not much is said as they put the canyons in the distance behind them. A little while later, ROJ points to his left as he swings his canoe to the river access. Upon beaching his canoe, the others line up theirs next to him.

ROJ finds his shuttle vehicle parked up above in the parking area. He motions for the others to begin unpacking their canoes while he retrieves the vehicle to start loading.

There is a sign of gratitude and exhilaration as they all begin unpacking their watertight bags and transferring their belongs to the suitcases they brought with them.

ROJ loads up his supplies first so the others can retrieve their belongings right away back in Lajitas. Once the canoes are emptied, the canoes are loaded onto the trailer for the trip back. On their way back, Weyland breaks the silence in the truck and says, "Well, ROJ, what's next for you?"

"I don't have to worry about time off or taking any vacation time because every day is a vacation for me. I have found through a set of extraordinary circumstances that this has become my life's pursuit. I'm truly doing what I love. Just have to wait around until the next river trip. Not sure when that will be," ROJ announces.

"You mentioned a set of extraordinary circumstances. Would I be out of line by asking what you mean?" Weyland asks.

"Not at all." ROJ is silent for a few seconds as if trying to collect his thoughts. In a crackling voice that obviously depicts he is stressed or nervous about something, he replies.

"I nearly died on this river after losing my parents and our guide in a flood surge. The gentleman who found me and saved my life is the guy I work with now. He's a river rat, and so am I now," ROJ explains. Without being too obvious, Weyland can see tears well up in ROJ's eyes. ROJ's driving becomes erratic for a few seconds, and he pulls over. "Will you all please excuse me for a few minutes?" ROJ opens the door and exits the truck. Walking around with his head bent over, the group can see he is truly distressed and wiping his eyes.

"Weyland, don't you think you should go to ROJ and say something?" Sierra breaks the silence.

"Yes, you are right. I'll see what I can do to help make things better for him."

Weyland exits the truck and gently walks over to ROJ. Placing a comforting hand on ROJ's shoulders as he comes up to him from behind, Weyland says,"ROJ, I can't imagine what you are experiencing right now, but I want you to know you are not alone in your pain. Sierra and Marcus have both lost one of their parents. They are very aware of how you need to express your sorrow and show respect for your parents' passing. We're in no hurry. You take as long as you need. We'll be waiting for you with open arms when you are ready go."

When Weyland open the truck door and takes his place in the front seat, Sierra already has tears in her eyes. "I can't imagine what ROJ has to go through knowing he lost his parents in a terrible accident. My Dad passed away from cancer, and that was bad enough for me."

"We all deal with sorrow and death of a family member in different ways. ROJ, he is reminded every trip what it is like when he passes the spot where the river took them away from him."

ROJ slowly walks back to the truck with his head held high wiping the remains of tears from his eyes. As he enters the truck and before turning on the ignition, he hears, "You are an extraordinary young man for a river guide," Weyland says. "You have a lot to be proud of. Very few of us find a form of employment we truly love. You are one of those, and I will always remember you when I think about loving what I do. The sorrows and tears you bear are a respectful reminder how important your parents were to you, and hopefully for the rest of your life."

As ROJ pulls away from the shoulder of the road, silence once again fills the inside of the shuttle. It's not long when the noise in the truck turns to normal chatter and shop talk as business matters surface. Nothing that interests ROJ even though he likes keeping abreast of all matters. Everything interests him to certain degrees. Entering the Lajitas city limits, the shuttle pulls up to where all their cars are parked. Getting out of the shuttle, everyone seems somewhat tired and relieved to make it back safely. ROJ watches while the shuttle is emptied. Sierra approaches him and gives him a big hug. "Thank you for a marvelous trip of a lifetime. I will tell all my friends."

"That is very kind of you. Thank you," ROJ replies.

Weyland walks up to ROJ, shakes his hand, and places a bill in his hand as he withdraws his. Without looking at it, ROJ places it in his pocket and responds with an approving nod. "Love what you do, and do what you love," Weyland says. "I will remember you, ROJ."

CHAPTER TWENTY-TWO

They all wave goodbye as they drive off. ROJ parks the shuttle after unloading the canoes. He ties them behind his and begins the mile paddle back home to his camp. As he approaches camp, FAM is the first to see him. She yells to him when he's just yards from shore. "No sense untying those canoes, as swipe. You have another trip to get ready for. Our beloved leader wants to go over this one with you. Kind of special, he thinks."

"Right away, Your Highness," ROJ replies, trying not to aggravate her. Otherwise, further insults will follow.

ROJ beaches the canoes without untying them. FAM is busy preparing dinner, knowing ROJ may be late arriving. *That's a nice thing for her to do for a change,* ROJ thinks.

Hooty is busy chopping wood and stacking it in a big pile, and DBoR drags the limbs over to the fire before dressing the meat he shot for dinner. Upon entering the confines of ST's tent, ROJ asks about the next river trip.

"Got a message from Rachael pertaining to your next trip," ST says. "What do you mean, my next trip? Why don't you take it? You're more qualified."

"This one is special like FAM announced to you, because this gentleman asked for the guide with 'the funny name.' Didn't know what he was talking about until I went down the list of our camp occupants. You were recommended to him," ST says.

"Recommended by whom? Who do I know?"

"That's not the point, son. It's an honor to be recommended by anyone. Just accept it for what it is," ST replies.

"Well, give me the rundown so I can get started preparing for it tomorrow," ROJ asks.

"All I know is the person who booked this trip. His name is Ira Dresden, and he is coming with four other people. He said something about only having four to five days or so for this trip, so give them options before leaving with the shuttle. You have all day tomorrow to get ready and seal your meals in vacuum plastic bags. I'll inform FAM to keep the fire hot all day so you can prepare. Good luck with this one, ROJ," ST announces.

With that, ROJ collects himself, walks down to the fire, and has a delicious meal prepared by FAM. ROJ doesn't talk much at all during supper. His thoughts are swimming with what Weyland said to him upon leaving and going over meal menus in his mind for the next five-day trip. *Five meals times two times five days including lunch and finger food. Wine. Don't forget about the wine. One gallon per day.*

Finally, ROJ begins getting drowsy. After finishing supper, he walks straight for his tent, unzips the entrance and disappears.

The next morning when ROJ crawls out of his tent, the smell of coffee and breakfast on the skillet is hard to ignore. As he walks over to the fire, FAM is there with her normal abusive behavior. "Well, look what the cat drug up. You really look like shit today."

"Thank you for those kind words. You look wonderful yourself," ROJ replies. "Your breakfast really smells great. Don't know what we would do without you, FAM."

ROJ is so busy consuming the delicious breakfast FAM has assembled and preparations swimming in his head, he doesn't even notice the further insults FAM throws at him. After being ignored several times, FAM finally gets the message and leaves ROJ alone. Enjoying this quiet solitude may be the only rest he will get for the rest of the day. Preparing for his next river trip tomorrow is going to command his total attention all day, and possibly the night. Sipping his coffee and slowly tasting every bite, he hears bird songs everywhere, the subtle crackle of the fire, and constant mesmerizing sound of the river. ROJ almost falls asleep.

Catching himself while nearly doubling over with his eyes closed, he realizes it's time to get started before he goes back to his tent to sleep some more.

When ST got word of the next river trip from Rachael that was recommended for ROJ, he canoed into town to pick up all the supplies he knew ROJ would need. He picked up flank steak that would be cooked into bite-size cubes for a variety of meals, sirloin steak to put directly on the grill, bacon, sausage, eggs, potatoes, bread, cheese, canned and fresh vegetables, supplies to replenish his gorp, other nonperishable food, and of course, five gallons of wine. All this ST put into storage for ROJ to use.

ST takes care of his people, and he knows how to take care of his customers to make sure that they truly have the experience of a lifetime. He is truly the leader of the river rats. He knew ROJ would not have time to run into town himself and get all the preparations done in one day. His compassion that he hides very well comes out in the most subtle ways, but when it does show, it makes a statement.

ROJ walks up to the storage building with his list in hand and grabs the meat out of cold storage he will need for many of his evening meals. It takes several trips for him to assemble all the food ST supplied for him, and he begins by cooking the flank steak, cutting it into bite-size cubes to make into beef stroganoff and beef stew. These will be put into plastic containers and vacuum sealed to be reheated in hot water. He does the same for the canned veggies in order to minimize weight from taking the cans along. Once all the meals are prepared and sealed, everything is carefully assembled in several coolers and packed with ice.

All of the cooking and meal preparations take ROJ well into early evening. He doesn't even take time to eat. FAM realizes how zoned- in ROJ is all day, so she prepares a simple evening meal that he could eat consisting of beef stew, potatoes, and vegetables. No insults are exchanged by FAM, which is out of the ordinary. Somehow, she realizes how exhausted ROJ is and how important this next trip is to him. She simply smiles and nods while ROJ inhales his food then disappears into his tent. All is silent for the rest of the evening.

The next morning, ROJ awakes to another delicious smell in the air. FAM is busy making breakfast which consists of his favorite: eggs over easy, hash brown potatoes with gravy and sausage. He remembers in his former life how disgusting this breakfast was to him, but this is his new life now, and this breakfast has taken center stage as being his favorite for some reason. Maybe because he now lives in the open, and everything tastes better when cooked over a fire especially the way FAM cooks it.

"It's about time you piece of shit got up. I was about to barge into your tent to roll out your ass," FAM says with her normal smirk. With hearing that, ROJ knows everything is normal and all is good.

"I love you too," ROJ says with half a smile on his face. "Your breakfast is always worth getting up for, no matter what time."

FAM's insults no longer bother ROJ, and he has become accustomed to hearing them. It has become quite comical preparing himself to receiving them. In fact, he doesn't know what the river rat lifestyle would be like without her insults. It's a unique quality of life of being a river rat, and he would not trade it for anything.

After enjoying every morsel of FAM's cooking, ROJ is energized and full of determination. What a glorious day to look forward to. He loads up all his supplies in his canoe, including lifejackets, ties two other canoes to his, and begins the canoe trip to town to meet his new customers. Upon arriving, he beaches the two other canoes and assembles the oars and lifejackets in an organized fashion. Walking up the beach a short ways, he sees of group of five lost souls pondering what will happen next. ROJ walks up the group and introduces himself. "Hello, my name is ROJ. Which one of you is Ira Dresden?"

Ira identifies himself, and ROJ continues by saying, "It's a pleasure to meet you. I will be your guide. Would you please identify the rest of your group, Ira."

"Yes, ROJ, I'll be glad to. This gentleman with the short curly afro is Aydin Haskell. This striking young woman is Madeline Harley Meriweather. She doesn't like either of her names, so she goes by H&M. This gentleman with the long hair is Phillip Scranton, and last but not least is Skye Donahue. Every three months or so H&M and Skye secretly dye their hair before coming to work to see if they wind up with matching colors. They have succeeded only once to my knowledge," Ira announces.

"It's a pleasure to meet you all. I was told you have just four to five days for this river trip experience. Can you tell me what you know about the canyons of the Rio Grande?" ROJ asks.

"Actually, ROJ, we don't know anything about the Rio Grande. Would please explain to us what you recommend?" Ira says.

"First of all, how many of you have whitewater experience?" ROJ inquires. Everyone shakes their heads no. "OK, then, I want to describe the upper and lower canyons so you can all decide which section you would like to canoe."

"That would be the most helpful, ROJ. We are putting our trust in you in order to accommodate our inexperience," Ira replies.

"Since you have only four to five days, the Colorado and Santa Elena canyons will take four to five days to canoe. You can also put in just past Santa Elena to canoe the Mariscal and Boquillas. Those two canyons will also take about five days. The Mariscal has some very challenging rapids, and the Boquillas is completely flat water. It can be quite boring but is also beautiful. Now the lower canyons consists of constant rapids of class II and III. In higher water levels, they can escalate to class IV. There's not much rest between each rapid, and they should be canoed only by experienced canoeists," ROJ explains.

"Thank you for that descriptive breakdown, ROJ. It sounds like the Colorado and Santa Elena are very similar to the Mariscal and Boquillas, expect that the first two are closer. I hope I speak for everyone by saying the Colorado and Santa Elena would accommodate us the best," Ira says. His decision is followed by nods of approval by the rest of the group.

"Very well then. We will begin with the Colorado. While you all get your luggage, I will back up the shuttle and trailer down to the beach," ROJ says. He walks to the parking lot where the shuttle truck is located with the canoe trailer. The crossbars of the trailer can accommodate up to six canoes comfortably. He pulls around and backs down the trailer to the beach, making loading the canoes easier. As soon as ROJ is set, the group walks up to him with their luggage.

"If you would please help me load the canoes, you can put your luggage in the back."

After everything is loaded, ROJ drives the group to Redford, where they will put in. The drive is a short half-hour trip. ROJ notices their eyes are fixated on the river. Everyone muttering all at once sounds like undetectable chatter. He just smiles knowing that they will enjoy the simplest of challenges. Arriving to Redford, ROJ makes his way to the put in by the river. He backs up the trailer and instructs the group to exit. "Please help me unload the canoes onto the beach, and I will go over all the instructions before we begin," ROJ says.

As the group takes out their luggage, ROJ lays out five yellow bags on the ground.

"What are those for?" Skye asks.

"These are waterproof bags where all your belongings will be transferred from your luggage into these bags. It takes a little bit of time, so pack the bags carefully, making sure you take with you everything you want for the next five days."

It's quite a humorous display watching the group stuffing their belongings into the bags not knowing how to assemble their stuff. The guys are not as delicate as the girls, and what seems like twenty minutes feels like an hour.

"OK. Please bring your bags by the canoes, and I'll show you how to pack your canoes since you all will be doing this by yourselves after this. First, I want you to put on your lifejackets since you will be wearing these during the entire trip while you are on the water," ROJ explains. ROJ then continues to explain the different parts of the canoes and the different strokes of the oars. The spiel he uses with this group has become repetitive from the former river trips. ROJ returns the shuttle and trailer to the parking lot to be driven to the take-out at the Santa Elena River Access by someone else in Redford.

CHAPTER TWENTY-THREE

ROJ instructs the group how to pack their canoes, then they all push off. "The Colorado has more rapids than any other canyon on the Rio Grande, but they are all small and very enjoyable. They will give you good practice for the class II and III you will encounter in the Santa Elena," ROJ announces. Ira instructs Skye to ride with ROJ while he and Aydin ride in the stern of the two other canoes.

"How do you figure our time on these two canyons?" Ira asks.

"We will spend the first two days on the Colorado, then take the five rapids in the Santa Elena slowly and carefully." "Do you really think we really have what it takes to float those class III rapids?" Phillip asks.

"Of course I do. You will be pleasantly surprised how well equipped you will be to tackle those rapids on day three. Just leave it to me to train you, but you have to follow my instructions so I can ensure your safety," ROJ replies.

"We'll do whatever you ask, ROJ," H&M shouts from the farthest canoe.

As they quietly and peacefully paddle with the gentle current of the Colorado, ROJ notices everyone looking around, observing along the bank, listening to the sounds, and watching for life. He can tell that these novices have not spent much time in the great outdoors. ROJ lets them soak in all that is around them. This is their experience. They need to absorb all they can in their own ways. A short time later, Skye announces, "What's that roaring sound, ROJ?"

"That's your first set of rapids. They will all announce themselves like that. The larger rapids will, of course, be louder, but that will come later."

As they become closer to the first rapid, ROJ instructs them to follow him through the notch. "Remember, in order to control your speed, back paddle until you feel comfortable enough to paddle with the current. It will take each of you a different amount of time to reach that point."

ROJ enters the notch, followed by Ira then Aydin. As ROJ looks back at their progress, Ira's canoe is doing great while Aydin is back paddling hard, slowing his progress and making his discomfort obvious. Hitting slack water past the first rapid, Ira follows in no time. They all wait in quiet respect while Aydin makes it through the rapid. A smile does not appear on his face until the stress of the first rapid wears off. Then a huge smile finally makes it mark, and everyone laughs and yells at his success. That proves to be just the support Aydin needs in order to float the remaining rapids of the first day.

"We are getting close to the tinaja, a spring-fed water pool, where you can get out and swim or explore. After we get through these next set of rapids, we can beach the canoes for lunch. The remaining rapids are just as simple and enjoyable. H&M seems to be having the most fun by waving her oar above her head and screaming and laughing. ROJ sees Ira just shaking his but smiling at the same time.

"Follow me over to that beach where the tinaja is, and I'll get lunch ready," ROJ announces.

After beaching the canoes, Skye and H&M are the first to strip down to their swimsuits. Skye is wearing a sleek two- tone one-piece swimsuit while H&M flaunts her figure with a skimpy bikini radiating in bright red. Both of Skye and H&M were college friends, participated on the same volleyball team, and attended a lot of the same classes. Being fitness oriented has kept their curves and muscle tone striking, something the guys can't help staring at. As they make their way over to the tinaja, all eyes are peeled and on them until they disappear into the water. The silence is broken by screams, "Wow, this water is cold as a witch's butt!" Skye yells. "Hey, come on in. It doesn't take long to get used to it!"

Phillip says, "You don't have to ask me twice." Ira and Aydin shake their heads and continue hiking over the small ridge. When the three emerge from the tinaja thirty minutes later for lunch, their lips and fingernails have turned purple. "It's cold, but what a rush. That will definitely wake you up," H&M replies.

ROJ has assembled a spread of sandwiches, potato salad and coleslaw, cheese and crackers, and some deli meat. Ira and Aydin show up and are amazed at the lunch ROJ has for them. "This is no simple lunch—this is a gourmet meal," Aydin says. "Is this something we will have for every lunch?" "This and more. I aim to please. This is your trip, and I want every part of it to be a memorable experience."

155

"Well, if you mean through our stomachs, then you are on the right track," Ira says.

While they all stuff their faces with a delicious lunch, the guys can't stop peering at the girls sitting and standing in their swimsuits. "Instead of dressing again, I think I'll canoe the rest of the day like this," Skye announces.

"No complaints from me," Phillip says. "Down, boy," Aydin says. Skye takes it as a compliment and just smiles.

As they continue through a set of four more rapids, ROJ looks over to the other canoes where there is a lot of hooping and hollering going on. They are truly having a great time. ROJ knows that confidence will come in handy when they hit Santa Elena. "Follow me to that beach up on the left. As soon as we beach, untie your supplies, and I'll show you how to set up your tents so you'll know how to do it yourselves the next time," ROJ says.

Following ROJ's instructions, they unpack their canoes and lay out everything on the ground. "OK, follow me as I set up my tent. That way, you will know how to help each other. Then, you can throw your gear in and set up your sleeping bags," ROJ announces.

After helping ROJ set up his tent, the others begin helping one another while ROJ gets a fire started. He then unpacks two coolers with enough supper supplies to feed an army. When the fire roars to life, he places the grill first, then fills up two big pots with fresh water used for boiling and bringing the sealed food packs to life. As ROJ sets up his supplies, the group begins to join him at the fire.

"So, ROJ, what is this surprise you have in store for us tonight?" Skye asks.

He reaches behind one of the coolers and pulls out a gallon of wine. "Why don't you begin with this as I explain what is in store for you?"

Their eyes shoot wide open, not believing the quantity of wine they are seeing. Laughter starts up as the bottle and cups makes their way around the circle. "For supper, your first night consists of sirloin steak, baked potatoes smothered with butter, heated assorted vegetables, and for dessert, cheesecake with your choice of toppings."

"ROJ, dang. How do you assemble such a gourmet meal outdoors on the river with no facilities?" H&M asks.

"You'd be surprised what any of you could do with a little bit of ingenuity," ROJ replies.

"I think it might be wise to pace ourselves with this wine until we eat something," Ira suggests. The group nods with approval.

As ROJ turns the steaks and the aroma fills the air, everyone licks their lips. Skye asks what everyone is thinking, "How much longer, ROJ? You are truly making us very hungry."

"Give me five more minutes with these steaks. Since the baked potatoes are already partially cooked and the water is boiling with the veggies, I would say ten minutes, tops," ROJ says.

The group grabs their plates, and while sitting around the fire on logs left over from the last trip, ROJ begins by placing a huge eight-ounce steak on each plate. A baked potato follows with a big slab of butter. ROJ then cuts open the sealed bags of assorted veggies and places a big helping on each plate. "There's more for everyone, so don't be bashful for seconds." The only word that breaks the silence of people stuffing their faces with delicious gourmet food is "Incredible," which Ira exclaims.

As Phillip is the first to finish his plate of food, he announces, "I can tell already, ROJ, that you aim to spoil us." "Hopefully, that is my plan. It's all part of the whole experience."

"Just incredible," Ira announces again helping himself to seconds.Several are through with their plates of food, and ROJ breaks out the chilled cheesecake. "I hope you left enough room for dessert because this cheesecake will not make it another day. It's now or never."

As everyone sighs from stuffing themselves, ROJ dishes up a slice of dessert whether they want one or not. No one digs in right away. It takes ten to fifteen seconds before anyone touches it. But, when H&M is the first to eat, she can't eat it fast enough. The joy on her face is overwhelming, so the others begin eating. Within minutes, all the dessert is gone. "Incredible," Ira says for a third time.

"Don't you have anything else to say, Ira?" Aydin says. "It's the only word I need."

As ROJ finishes his meal, a smile fills his face as he tries not to let the others see. The others break out the wine and continue laughing and telling stories while ROJ begins cleaning up. "By the way, ROJ, what time do we get under way in the morning?" Skye asks.

"Why are you thinking about that already? Just enjoy the rest of supper and this delicious wine. I'm sure ROJ will tell us when he's ready," Aydin replies.

"Actually, I'll have coffee ready and breakfast started before any of you even consider rolling out of bed. Don't worry. I'll take care of everything," ROJ says.

"I can tell already that you are most capable of doing anything you want," Ira replies.

CHAPTER TWENTY-FOUR

A s the jug of wine gets close to empty and everyone turns their chatter to business, Ira leads the discussion of why they booked this trip in the first place. While ROJ cleans up, he pours himself the remaining cup of wine. He overhears Ira and rest talking about their investment scenario and how long it will take to contract out all the different parts that are needed to make a presentation to the bank. ROJ hears Aydin mention something about a golf course community, and his ears perk up. "Please forgive me, sir, for interrupting, and I beg your permission for saying so, but I overheard you all talking about a golf course community."

"Yes, ROJ, that is correct. Is there something I can help you with?" Ira asks.

"I heard you mention the array of disciplines involved in creating a design and all the specs necessary to assemble in order to present to your bank."

"Yes, that's correct," Ira replies.

"If I may continue, I think I can help that may relieve some of the problems you are facing that can save you some time," ROJ states.

"ROJ, what can you do to save us time? What kind of special talents do you have that could be of any benefit to us?" Phillip asks.

"If you would be kind enough to allow me to look at what you have, I think I can have something ready for you by morning that will prove that to you."

As Ira turns his head to the side, away from everyone else, he produces a smile of approval. "I wonder what else he knows, indeed," Ira says under his breath.

The group looks at Ira for some type of response, and with a slight approving nod from H&M, Ira says, "All right, ROJ. Let me get you what we brought with us, and you can do whatever you think you can. You can show me in the morning if what you come up with will be helpful to us."

"ROJ, why do you want to do this?" Skye asks.

"It's something to do to expand my mind and keep me busy."

While Ira hunts down the paperwork and schematic layouts for the project, the rest of them start walking toward their tents. Ira displays a huge blueprint that exhibits a layout of the land on which the project will be. The tract of land is enormous—roughly one and a half square miles, about nine hundred acres. It also includes all existing vegetation. He also gives ROJ a multitude of transparent layouts the same size of the blueprint with information pertaining to contour (elevation) lines, soil types, and geological information pertaining to subsoil structures such as underground springs/aquifers; rock formations, etc.; water/utility lines; and right of ways.

"I'm glad you came so equipped with all this information.

All of it is important with nothing left out," ROJ says.

Ira was surprised that ROJ didn't even flinch when he was given the multitude of charts and layouts. As he walks toward his tent, he says while looking over his shoulder, "I'm looking forward to being surprised in the morning. Give me your best shot, ROJ."

With that, Ira disappears in his tent.

The next morning, Ira rolls out of his tent to the smell of freshly brewed coffee and breakfast on the griddle. "I think I could live with that smell for the rest of my life. What do you have cooked on the skillets, ROJ?" Ira inquires.

"A hearty breakfast fit for kings and queens. I'm hoping the smell of food will wake up everyone else. Until then, please indulge," ROJ responds.

"Don't you think there are a lot of coals for one breakfast?" Ira asks. "I needed light from a big fire to work on your project last night." "You mean, you actually did work on it? I thought you were just kidding," Ira says half jokingly.

"Yes, and I got a lot done. Can't wait to show you," ROJ excitedly replies. "Do you want me to show you or your whole group?"

"I'd rather wait until more are awake," Ira says.

While Ira gorges down on coffee and a classic farmer's breakfast, their talking and laughing wake up everyone else. Aydin is the first to appear. His tight, curly afro looks like he never slept on it. Phillip's long, shoulder-length hair combs out easily as does Skye's beautiful long blonde hair. H&M's curly strawberry-blond hair looks like a bird took up residency over night. Phillip is the first to poke fun at her. "Be careful not to disturb your new resident when you try to get a comb through that bird's nest of yours."

She just throws a smirk in his direction, then joins everyone else at the fire. "ROJ cooked up a hearty breakfast fit for kings and queens. Eat up before it all gets cold," Ira announces.

"I heard you two talking before any of us rolled out of our tents. You said you have something to show us, ROJ?" Aydin says.

"Yes, I do. While you eat your fill, I'll get the layouts," ROJ says. ROJ walks into to his tent and returns with a bundle of huge layouts piled on top of one another. "As you finish breakfast and drink up the remaining coffee, I'll get started with what I was able to accomplish last night. It will help if I begin by explaining the procedure I used before actually showing the results. I think that would eliminate a few questions."

"I began by placing the blue print on the ground that has a layout of the entire property you plan to develop. It has all existing vegetation and structures on it. I then placed the first transparent layout of all geological structures on top of it. This gave me a clear picture of what lies beneath, thus, avoiding extensive construction costs on your part. Next, I placed on top of that the transparent layout of existing water and utility lines, thus, avoiding further extensive construction costs. Utility companies can move certain utilities for a predetermined cost instead of paying for unnecessary construction costs and delays. Next, I placed the soil composition layout so I would know what type of soil would support certain types of digging and construction. Last, I placed the transparent layout of contour/elevation lines

163

indicating the slope of the land and drainage. My design for your golf course was drawn on top of the last layout in light pencil," ROJ explains.

"How do you know to do all that in precise sequence?" Skye asks. Without answering, ROJ continues. "Before designing a golf course, I took into consideration the location around the perimeter where 240 house lots could possibly be located. The sale of these lots is where you will make back your initial investment and give you the quickest returns. From there, any golf course design originates around three precisely located holes—holes 1, 9, and 18. Every serious golfer knows that there is an unwritten rule of where these three holes should be located on any golf course. I carefully positioned them where they would complement the entrance and club house of your golf course community. Any challenging golf course should have at least three par 3 holes, two Hail Mary holes of five hundred yards or longer located on the front and back nine, and the rest comprised of average skill and length. The true challenge comes in designing narrow straightaways and dog legs with restrictive landscaping and sand traps."

"Is that all?" H&M asks.

"No. I made an educated guess as to the entrance based on existing roads or right aways and where the least amount of road construction would take place according to the original blueprint," ROJ says.

"Incredible," Skye replies.

"All of this I have explained to you so far is just the preliminary setup."
"You mean to say there's more?" H&M states.

"Of course. Now let me show you. Using a bubble design that landscaper designers use to mark out specific usage of plant materials, I used that technique to first mark out the perimeter of where the house lots would be located. As you can see here, the location of holes 1, 9, and 18 are located in specific locations on the total design. Everything else was designed around them. The straight and dog leg lines indicate the center of fairways with the rectangles being the tee boxes and the circles being an approximate shape of the greens. I was able to add sand traps to add to the challenge of each hole based on existing vegetation. The creek and pond make for an easy challenge that works for certain holes. All the remaining holes can become more difficult by introducing additional plantings and obstacles. Usually, trees are used to increase or decrease the skill needed to conquer each hole. Tomorrow, I can actually design the dimensions of each house lot and incorporate additional landscaping ideas."

"I have never seen anything more amazing in my life for one night's work," Ira proudly exclaims. "The work you have completed, ROJ, even without looking at the property or consulting with engineers, general contractors, or the USGS, is nothing short of genius." Others nod in agreement and surprise. "This work of yours, if applicable, just saved us six to nine months of time and expense. I can't wait to see what you come up with tomorrow."

"I think you should put this information someplace safe and dry, Ira, until we make camp tonight. Tomorrow, we enter Santa Elena where things can get wet," ROJ advises.

As they all finish up breakfast and begin taking down camp, ROJ shows the group how to fold up his tent so they can all help one another. Once they are finished packing their watertight bags and sleeping bags, ROJ is finished breaking down breakfast and loading supplies in his canoe. He shows them how to pack each canoe and checks their ropes when done. The amount of water he has to use to drown the fire pit would signal an army fifty miles away.

CHAPTER TWENTY-FIVE

A
s they shove off, ROJ says, "The rest of today is a repeat of yesterday, easy paddling and small rapids. You could easily make it to the Santa Elena Canyon by late afternoon if you all push hard, but I honestly suggest you rest up tonight before tackling Santa Elena. Enjoy yourselves today and the sights and sounds, and we can camp comfortably before beginning the bigger rapids tomorrow."

"ROJ, what do you mean by the bigger rapids?" H&M asks apprehensively.

"The rapids on the Santa Elena are somewhat bigger than those of the Colorado because the canyon is more narrow, squeezing the water. That, accompanied with obstacles in the river, make for faster rapids. I really think you will be ready. Just enjoy yourselves and relax. After a few more rapids, you'll be entering the chutes, then we'll stop for lunch while beachfront property is still easy to find," ROJ explains.

Less than an hour later, Aydin asks ROJ if he could take the lead into the next rapid. "Sure. Just hit the notch head-on." Paddling like he was a pro,

Aydin did just as ROJ suggested, and the rest of the group followed. Ira volunteered to lead the group through the next one. Ira and Aydin took turns leading each rapid. ROJ knew that building their confidence before entering Santa Elena was key to making the rest of the trip a success.

"Hey, it's time for lunch. Anyone hungry?" ROJ announces. "Are you kidding. I'm famished. I could eat anything!"

Skye yells for everyone.

"From our experience so far, ROJ doesn't just make anything for us. Every meal is gourmet," Phillip announces above the roar of the approaching rapid.

The two other canoes follow ROJ onto the beach. As they all exit their canoes, ROJ says, "It won't take me long to get lunch ready, but walk around and explore for a short while. Be back here shortly."

Skye and H&M take off in one direction, Phillip and Aydin take off in another, and Ira stays with ROJ. "Anything I can help you with, ROJ?" Ira asks.

"Not really, Ira. However, you can see if you can find any logs that the others can sit on."

Ira walks around and doesn't find anything. "Oh well. I guess they can sit in their canoes," ROJ says.

While ROJ unpacks just the right cooler chest and lays out a beautiful spread of sandwiches, cheese, pickles, chips, gorp, and finger food, Ira is amazed at how organized and efficient ROJ is spreading out everything and in a clean and appealing manner. Somehow, he can find a way to make any meal look appealing no matter the terrain.

It's not long before the others begin to show up. The way they rummage through the food laid out for them, one would think that they are famished and undernourished. Apparently, the seating arrangement is no problem. They grab food and eat as fast as they can. Ira is just as amazed as ROJ is in the way the lunch supplies are devoured.

"That is truly one amazing luncheon, ROJ. Can't imagine how you pulled it off, considering the terrain. You are amazing," Skye says delightfully.

"You're welcome. Every step of the way, especially when food is involved, it's my job to make your experience the best ever," ROJ replies.

"You know what, so far, you have surpassed any expectations I ever had of this river trip adventure. Don't know what any of us would do without you, ROJ," H&M says.

"Thank you. You are too kind. I aim to please."

When everyone has consumed their fill, ROJ packs up lunch, and they push off. This time, Skye asks to row in the stern with ROJ in the bow. The next rapid can be heard just around the bend, and Skye asks to take the lead.

"Skye, are you sure you want to take lead?" Ira asks. "Since we are practicing with these small rapids, sure. I'm ready."

"Don't worry, Ira. Just follow us through," ROJ says.

Skye aligns the canoe just right to shoot the notch and enters with no problem. "Skye, there's a sizable boulder in this one rapid. I'm going to reach left, so you need to paddle hard on the right. Start now!" ROJ yells to her over the roar of the water.

As ROJ looks back, Skye is following his directions just fine. She is maintaining speed with the current and turning the canoe around the boulder. He further looks farther back and notices the other canoes following suit. ROJ then yells back to Skye to begin paddling hard on the left as he reaches right to finalize their turn around the boulder. ROJ reaches hard and makes it to the eddy, waiting to see how the others make it around safely. They do, and he and Skye follow them through to flat water.

"Wow. What a rush! I never knew it could be so exciting to be in control going through a rapid," Skye shouts.

"Don't let it go to your head, my dear. I think these small rapids are just the beginning of our adventure. Enjoy it while you can. A different fate awaits us tomorrow," Ira says.

"What does he mean by that, ROJ?" Skye inquires.

"It's just that the rapids become more challenging in Santa Elena, so do the very best you can today. I'm going to need everything you've got tomorrow," ROJ replies. As he looks back, Skye give him a huge approving nod.

Rapid after rapid and Skye remains a trooper, attacking the notch and paddling on the opposite side as ROJ. The rapids are small, and ROJ can hear Skye hollering with every minute accomplishment above the roar of the water. This is exactly the type of energy she is going to need in order to tackle the five rapids of Santa Elena.

170

ROJ motions for Skye to move closer to the rest of the canoes.

"Hey, how about lunch?"

"Exactly what I was thinking, or at least, what my stomach was thinking," Phillip speaks up for everyone.

"There's a flat area where we can beach the canoes. It's not big, but it's large enough for us to get out safely," ROJ says.

As the canoes are beached, ROJ announces, "Take time to walk around. It won't take long for me to set up lunch."

H&M hangs around while ROJ sets up lunch. "I would like to take the stern for the rest of the day while we have small rapids left. Can you help me, ROJ?"

"That's between you and Ira to work that out. I can't interfere," ROJ replies.

"He can be a bit controlling even though he is a nice guy. What if he says no?"

"What if he says yes?" ROJ politely bolsters. "You won't know if you don't give it a try. Remember, H&M, if you want the responsibility of controlling your canoe by being in the stern, you have to act the part. That's what Ira would expect. Nothing less."

H&M looks down at the ground and nods in agreement. ROJ could tell she was trying to find her inner strength. Lunch was set up quickly, and ROJ says to H&M, "You need to eat if you want your strength to tackle the stern position. You have to decide when you want to ask Ira, so fill up, enjoy the sandwiches."

H&M begins stuffing her face as the rest of the group approaches over a small ridge.

"Hey, save some for us!" Aydin yells as they get closer. "H&M, I know you have told me on many occasions that you want more responsibility at the office and helping out more with customer presentations. Perhaps, this is a perfect time to prove that you can tackle adversity when it's thrown in your court. You take the stern for the rest of the afternoon, if that's all right with you," Ira commands.

H&M peers right at ROJ, and with a huge smile that covers her entire face, she replies to Ira, "I was going to ask you just that. I'm glad we are thinking on the same wavelength. I would be glad to take the stern. Thanks."

H&M looks in ROJ's direction again ever so slightly, and ROJ gives her an approving nod. The smile still consumes her face as she finishes lunch.

"I saw probably a dozen different bird species during our short walk. Who would think that in this barren but beautiful landscape that there is so much life?" Aydin says.

"There's life all around. Most people don't take the time to look for it or sit quietly and allow it to announce itself. I'm glad you took notice. It's all part of the whole experience,"

ROJ pleasingly says. "During spring, there are more than four hundred bird species in the Big Bend park, and it becomes a birder's paradise. Those brave souls who tackle a big year know that Big Bend is a must in order to boost their life list."

"Incredible. Who would have thought."

"ROJ, these sandwiches are absolutely delicious. I honestly think you make a gourmet meal out of anything. What do you have in store for us tonight?" Phillip says.

"Besides the wine?"

"Yes, besides the wine, even though I am looking forward to that as well."

"How about grilled chicken breasts, mashed potatoes and gravy, veggies, and more cheesecake?"

"That sounds wonderful!" Skye shouts in excitement. "How much time do we have before we run out of the Colorado?" Ira asks.

"In just a few hours. As we approach the tall canyons of Santa Elena, darkness will come earlier, and you all will need your strength for the class II and III tomorrow," ROJ replies.

"Can the class of a rapid change?" H&M asks.

"Yes. As the water level changes, so does the classification of the rapid. If we're lucky, the water level will remain low for the next few days," ROJ explains.

"What do you mean, 'if we're lucky,' ROJ?" Skye uncomfortably asks. "While we are in the Santa Elena Canyon, the walls are very tall with no beaches to reach high ground. As long as the water level remains constant, we will be just fine. So don't worry."

"What if the water level does rise while we are in the canyons?" Skye persists.

ROJ tries to ignore her as he cleans up and packs the remaining lunch supplies in the cooler. "Everyone get ready. We are about to push off so we can make the next beach area with sunlight left."

Skye gives ROJ an uneasy stare as ROJ walks through the canoe, allowing Skye to take the stern seat. Going through the next small rapid, Skye is quiet, as if in deep thought. She begins to loosen up with the next rapid, knowing it's futile to think about something for which she has no control.

After successfully floating through several more rapids, ROJ announces, "We will be coming up on the chutes soon. I think you all have enough confidence to shoot the chutes. As we get close, there may be a line of canoes waiting to go through. Just follow my lead, and I think you will all have a lot of fun with them."

ROJ's words are accurate. As they creep upon the the chutes, there are a dozen or more canoes lined up to encounter the chutes. As ROJ turns around, there is a sense of excitement on the faces of the group. He now knows they are finally ready to accept challenges. Watching the other canoes go through, it looks like a piece of cake. Finally, ROJ and Skye enter the first chute. With oars lifted above their heads, the current thrusts them through within seconds. Ira and H&M enter the first chute. Instead of lifting their oars above their heads, H&M tries to paddle. Her oar gets stuck along the side of the canoe, slowing their passage through the chute. At least they do not stop, but the current is powerful enough to move them along. Finally, they clear the chute so they can watch Aydin and Phillip go through. Phillip lifts his oar straight above his head while Aydin is somewhat more hesitant. He rests his oar on his lap ready to use it if needed. The current takes control of his canoe pushing it along scraping and jerking as it hits the sides of the chute. Aidin resists using his oar even though his face shows the contorted uneasiness of his situation. Before he and Phillip know it, they are through and receiving cheers and yells from the people lining the bank.

The second chute is just as fun as the first, and everyone goes through with their oars proudly lifted high above their heads. There are people everywhere lining both sides of the chutes cheering and screaming support at they shoot the chute. ROJ announces it's time to rest and make camp. They follow him to the beach. Skye says, "Are there usually this many people here?"

"Yes, this a very popular place. At times, here may be as many as one hundred canoeists or more. Many make a day trip out of these chutes," ROJ says. "This is a good time to get out and walk up toward the chutes to watch others go through. Before you all go exploring or cheering others going through the chutes, let's make camp. Follow me downstream another one hundred yards, and after your tents are set up, I'll work on starting a fire for supper.

The group beaches their canoes, unload everything, and begin setting up their tents. ROJ does the same, then goes back to his canoe to unpack the multitude of kitchen supplies. Getting supper set up takes a lot more effort than does breakfast. He roams the area in search of firewood. After he has assembled enough to last most of the evening, he starts the fire. By that time, the group have gone exploring. H&M and Skye walk toward the chutes to watch others go through. It is amazing how clean most canoeists shoot the chutes waving their oars above their heads and shouting like little kids. "The next time we have a long weekend, this is where I want to come to spend the day or more than one," H&M says to Skye.

"I'm with you. What a blast this would be especially with a little higher water," Skye replies.

The guys head off in another direction. Their location is revealed when Phillip lets out a high pitched scream. "Snake! More than one!" Phillip stepped on a sage brush bush that exploded in a series of rattles. With several rattlesnakes coiled up in his very near vicinity, Ira is the one who says, "Don't move a muscle, and, Aydin, go get ROJ now."

Aydin reaches ROJ and informs of the situation. He immediately takes a couple of smoking branches from the fire and runs toward Phillip. When he sees Phillip frozen with fear and not knowing what to do, ROJ says, "The snakes are all on one of you. As soon as I sneak these smoking branches in front of them, I will tell you when to run like hell, but not before. They can strike before you even twitch. Got it?"

"Yeah, ROJ. I got it," Phillip exclaims, trembling.

ROJ carefully places the smoking branches right in from of the snakes. One tries to strike the branch, but when the smoke confuses them and ROJ sees them back off just a hair, he says to Phillip, "Now, Phillip. Go!"

Phillip leaps from his position, falls flat on his face, gets up and begins running. No one was laughing, but the girls were snickering under their breath. "I think I've had enough exercise for now. ROJ, how about some of that wine?" Phillip says in relief to be alive.

"Sure thing. It's already out with cups set out for everyone," ROJ says.

They all make it back to camp and sit on the cool, sandy beach, sipping wine while watching ROJ get everything set up for supper. "So, ROJ, what's for supper?" Skye asks.

"I'm heating up mixed veggies in the hot water along with beef stroganoff. I'm getting ready to slap marinated chicken breasts on the grill. For dessert, there is apple pie. Hey, who wants to get started with making homemade ice cream?" ROJ asks.

"You've got to be kidding. Homemade ice cream out here in the middle of nowhere!" Aydin exclaims.

"For those of you who have not made it before, it takes quite a bit of effort. I didn't see an electrical plug in anywhere, so you'll have to do the old-fashioned way. I have the ingredients set up over there along with the rock salt. Good luck."

H&M takes off with the ice cream supplies and gets started turning the handle. It's not long before Skye has to step in to give H&M a breather. As soon as the chicken breasts are ready to take off the grill and the rest of supper is ready, ROJ sets up supper buffet style. The girls have finally finished making the ice cream, and they come back looking exhausted. "Got your workout for the day?" Ira asks.

"You bet. The next time is yours," H&M snaps back.

Sipping wine and stuffing their faces, no one is talking. "I guess that's a good thing," ROJ says under his breath. "There's plenty for seconds and thirds. Don't be bashful."

"You are truly incredible, ROJ!" Ira exclaims. "Another gourmet meal, wine, and if you couldn't top that, homemade ice cream out here. You are truly incredible."

"Every part of your trip, it's my job to make it as memorable as possible, including going through your stomachs," ROJ says.

"I think that is a very important part, if you ask me," Skye responds.

Everyone nods to that as faces are being stuffed with delicious food. "So what do you think was the most fun for you today, H&M?"

Aydin asks.

"Watching the expression of Phillip's face being surrounded by rattlesnakes."

"I mean, besides that?"

"I would say the chutes. I could probably to through them several times and never get tired of it," H&M replies.

"I'm with you there," Skye says.

"I didn't realize how quickly the sun went down with these canyon walls. It's dark already, and I never realized it at all," Phillip says.

"We were having so much fun, I don't think any of us noticed it," Ira replies.

"While you all finish the wine and stay up talking, Ira, would you please get those layouts I was working on yesterday?" ROJ asks.

"You going to work on them some more? You really do like doing that stuff, don't you?"

"I haven't had this much fun working on something like this in a while. It keeps my mind sharp and gives me a challenge," ROJ says.

"Very well. I'll get them for you," Ira says before walking to his canoe and pulling out the protected layouts. While the group enjoys one another's company around the huge fire, ROJ gets to work on the layouts. He continues long after the rest heat up to their tents and fall to sleep.

CHAPTER TWENTY-SIX

T he next morning, Ira is the first to emerge from the tents. "I told you once before, and I'll say it again. I could live with that smell of freshly brewed coffee every day for the rest of my life. I smell eggs and bacon as well. Everything you do, ROJ, is done to perfection. That's one thing I have noticed about you from the very beginning of our trip. It's a trait I don't see in my world very often. Thank you for that."

ROJ gives Ira a big nod of approval. The next to roll out of the tents is Aydin followed by H&M. "Food. I need substance. I need ROJ's cooking," H&M boasts. Within minutes, everyone is up and sitting around the fire on the cold sand.

"I don't know what will wake me up the most, ROJ's excellent cooking or this damn cold sand," Phillip says.

"You know, Phillip. If you want more meat to eat besides bacon and sausage, you can find a couple of snakes. I'm sure ROJ could prepare them for you," Skye replies.

"Very funny. You almost made me laugh."

"What does snake tastes like anyways?" Skye asks. Everyone looks at ROJ hoping he will have an answer.

"Each snake has its own unique flavor, but many taste like chicken."

With light laughter circulating around the group, Ira breaks in with a question. "Did you get any work done on those layouts last night, ROJ?"

"Yes, I did. Actually, quite a bit done since the design stage of the golf course itself was already done. Let me know when you're ready, and I'll show all of you.

"You all can keep eating, if you want. If you sit in a "U" shape in front of me, I think it would be easier for all of you to see better," ROJ says. He pulls out the layouts stacked on top of one another, and pins down the corners with small rocks. "If you notice, I finished the golf course design on the layout from yesterday.

"Around each hole, I included landscaping suggestions to accentuate the beauty. Each green area has a number of sand traps to add to the challenge. In the corner of this layout, I also included a cross sectional view of how the greens should be constructed. The depth of each green will depend on its size and the natural slope. If you look closely, each green is made up of ninety-five percent sand with tiles running along the bottom to disperse the accumulation of water as it percolates down through the green. The minimum depth of any green should be three to four feet with most being beyond six feet. Bent grass, of course, is the standard for greens mowed at less than three-sixteenths of an inch daily.

"The fairways are completely different. If you choose to use zoysia grass, which is easier to maintain at under two inches, it will be necessary to plant between twelve to fifteen acres of it as a backup in case it fails due to dry winter conditions, grubs, chinch bugs, or a sod webworm outbreak. It's maintenance schedule is a little different, requiring an aggressive aeration schedule to minimize thatch buildup that tends to choke itself out."

"Bluegrass is also commonly used that comes with its own problems. Being a high-maintenance grass, it needs lots of water, especially during the heat of the day. Grubs and sod webworms are very destructive to bluegrass. A heavy fungicide program is required to keep this grass green and untarnished during spring and summer months. Fall aeration helps keep it revitalized, just like with zoysia. Either way, groundskeeping managers have a lot to worry about in order to keep a golf course looking fantastic every single day."

"That is all amazing, so far, ROJ, but what are those geometric shapes all around the golf course?" Skye asks.

"I accommodated for 240 house lots which will give you the fastest returns on your investment. There are twenty lots closest to the Clubhouse that can sell for $120,000 each for a total return of $2.4 million. One hundred twenty lots located all around the fairways with some having more privacy and wildlife viewing than others can go for $100,000 each with a return of $12 million. The remaining lots, which are located behind and some off the course, can go for between $75,000 and $40,000 with an average $57,500 making that return of $5.75 million. So far, your initial nvestment return for lot sales total $20.15 million. Further income can be generated from a one-time initiation fee for golfers of $100,000. It's possible that only 60 percent of all homeowners will choose to play golf, so that investment return would be $14.4 million. Golf pro shop sales and tee fees are a source of daily income. An annual fee of $10,000 would be collected from all homeowners adding $2.4 million each year. Even for those homeowners who choose not to play golf at your golf course community, restaurant income will be a plus. Therefore, it would be safe to say that your investment return once all lots are sold could exceed $37 million. I know you have already looked into the value of the land you want to purchase, construction costs of the golf course itself, and an estimated cost of the club house and entrance road. You can easily determine how many years it will take you to get a complete return on your investment and how many years to take for you to start making serious money."

"You did all that last night?" Ira asks looking astounded. Everyone else had blank and confused stares on their faces.

"Yeah. What?" ROJ replies nonchalantly. "You did all that last night!" Skye repeats.

Jumping in, Aydin adds, "I think we all are astounded to the fact that what you have presented to us, ROJ, is nothing short of genius especially given the fact that all of this information represents just two nights of work. Do you have any idea how much time and expense you saved us by putting all this together?"

"No. Not really. I did this because it interests me, and being a challenge, it gives me something to do," ROJ says.

Ira interjects and says, "This work that you presented to us would take a professional company probably three to six months to assemble after they waste time with on-site inspections, surveying, calculations, design time amongst many individuals, and a team making a formal presentation to us. That is time and money lost. You are truly incredible, ROJ, and I think I speak for everyone here that it has been an honor to meet you and have you as our guide."

Ira then asks, "With that said, what is planned for us today?" "

After we leave here, there are a few more small rapids left before reaching Santa Elena. Have you noticed that the canyon walls are gettinghigher? When we do reach Santa Elena, the first rapid is called Matadero. Follow me through the notch, then paddle hard left to the eddy behind the big boulder on the left. I'll go over more instructions when reconvene there. Any questions?" ROJ says. With no response from anyone, ROJ continues and says, "Let's break camp and push off."

Once the canoes are loaded, they push off. The chatter is gleeful with normal laughter. The next small rapids are easy like the ones before, and everyone appears to have gained the confidence they need to tackle Santa Elena.

"Hey, ROJ. You were right. The canyon walls are huge," Skye says in amazement. "How tall do they get?"

"Once we enter the canyon, they will get up 1,500 feet tall. High enough to shorten our day of sunlight." ROJ pulls over toward the rest of them and says, "I want you to all put on game faces. These rapids are class II and III.

Michael E. Oppitz

The slight rise in water level overnight indicates that they may be closer to class III today. Any mistake in these rapids will not be as forgiving. Follow me through the notch, then paddle hard to the left to the eddy. I'll go over stage 2 with you from there." They get into single file like so many times before. ROJ shoots through the notch and immediately paddles hard on his right while Skye reaches hard on her left. His canoe remains parallel with the current, safely delivering them to the eddy. The next canoe through the notch is Aydin. He and H&M immediately start working their way toward ROJ on the left, and with no problem, they reach the eddy safely. Ira and Phillip are last to shoot the notch. As they shoot the notch, Ira's oar stumbles on a rock, making him lose his rhythm. With current pushing them hard, Ira has already lost two strokes, allowing the current to take him and Phillip where they don't want to go. Phillip is doing everything he can do by reaching hard on his left, but Ira can't get enough momentum paddling hard on his right. If they can't recover, they will go over the wall that jets out one third into the river, getting them caught in the undertow below—not to mention what will happen to their canoe. ROJ immediately escapes the safety of the eddy, propelling himself out into the current, racing toward them with all his might. With just feet between them and the rock wall, ROJ races past them, turns his canoe on a dime by back paddling hard on the left, and pivots himself around the stern of their canoe, putting him in position to get up against their canoe.

With all the strength ROJ can muster, he and Skye both paddle hard on the right, moving the two canoes parallel with the rock wall, still maintaining the same distance away from certain disaster. ROJ yells at Phillip to reach harder and faster. Within seconds of having the force of the current propel them over the wall, ROJ and Skye are able to turn the two canoes heading toward the big boulder. The eddy water grabs hold of the canoes, allowing them to make it to safety.

As soon as they reach the safety of the eddy and can relax, Phillip is already doubled over in exhaustion, shaking from the experience. Ira is also shaken, but to his credit, he maintains his composure. He extends his hand to ROJ, and ROJ notices it's shaking when he grabs it. "You saved our lives. You know that," Ira says in a crackling voice.

"Just doing my job," ROJ replies.

"How often does something like this happen?" Ira asks. "Every time is different, which is what makes it so interesting and exciting."

"I'm glad you think it's exciting, ROJ," Ira stutters. "I would use a different choice of words."

"Do you think this is something worth writing home about?" H&M interjects.

Ira says nothing but gives her a chuckle and an approving nod.

"We'll stay here as long as you need to. You let me know when you are ready," ROJ says.

A few moments later, Phillip straightens up, catching his breath and starts to calm himself. "I would classify this as a once-in-a-lifetime experience." That was enough to calm the mood and help the rest gather themselves.

"So ROJ, what's stage 2?" Skye asks.

"Stage 2 means we have to go back across that formidable rock wall again to the first notch you come to created by that other big boulder. This will be a lot easier this time since you just have to point your canoes in that direction and paddle like hell. Once you shoot the notch, back paddle hard on the right catching the eddy. Any questions?"

No one answers. They just fixate their eyes on the big boulder clear across the river. ROJ gives them some time to familiarize themselves with what they need to do. "Once again, watch what Skye and I do and repeat it without exception. Ready to paddle hard on the left, Skye?"

"You betcha. Just get me out there," she says without hesitation. ROJ back paddles catching the current. Skye begins paddling hard on the left like a trooper while ROJ does the same. The other two canoes watch as they fight the current but make good headway across the river toward their destination. As their canoe becomes parallel with the first notch, ROJ stops paddling and back paddles instead turning the canoe on a dime and into the notch. The current swallows them through. Then, with a huge back paddle on the right while Skye reaches on her right, the canoe swings around and into the safety of the eddy. "Easy as pie, huh, guys?" Ira says.

"Sure looks like it. ROJ makes everything look easy," H&M replies. "Come on, we can do this. Remember, without exception. Right?"

Without another word, Aydin turns his canoe into the current. He shouts encouragement to H&M to keep paddling hard on her left. In no time, they make it to the notch. As Aydin back paddles to turn the canoe into the notch, he does so too soon. The bow hits the end of the rock wall, and the stern is pushed up against the big boulder. Their canoe is stuck at a thirty degree angle against the current. Any second, the water can capsize them, crushing their canoe against the current and the boulder. H&M does something ROJ has never seen before. She reaches her oar straight ahead and somehow pushes the canoe just far enough away from the rock wall that the current is able to slide the canoe into the notch scraping the sides the entire way through. ROJ yells at Aydin, "Now, Aydin! Now!"

Aydin back paddles hard on his right, swinging the canoe into the safety of the eddy.

H&M says, "Can we go home now?"

"What do you mean? This is finally the fun part," Aydin says.

Skye turns around and looks at ROJ smiling at each other. Knowing that Ira and Phillip can't hear anything that is said over the roar of the rapid, Aydin waves them on. Ira nods, and before committing their canoe to the current, he says to

Phillip, "You ready to do this, buddy?" "Let's get it on, partner."

With serious determination on both their faces, Ira catches the current. Immediately, Phillip and Ira both start paddling hard on the left. Their canoe moves across the river parallel with the current like poetry in motion. Their strokes are precise with one another. With their canoe finally parallel with the first notch, Ira does exactly as instructed by back paddling hard on the left, sending them into falling water. He immediately changes sides with his oar, and while he's back paddling with all his might, the canoe responds to his will, swinging them into the safety of the eddy.

"I couldn't have done that any better myself," ROJ says breaking the tension. Ira nods his approval.

"Anyone hungry, yet?" ROJ asks.

"I think we all expended more energy than we thought. I know I'm hungry. Anyone else?" Ira asks.

Everyone nods yes. "Without making any sudden moves knocking us out of the eddy, I'll get some sandwiches, cheese, GORP, and finger food ready. Just relax for a while," ROJ says.

He gets out lunch and places it on the lid of the cooler to pass back and forth between the three canoes. With the danger in the past, small chatter and laughter finally return to their conversations. They are enjoying themselves again, and it shows on their faces.

As everyone is enjoying their lunch, ROJ speaks up and says, "I know some of you may be shaken from today's near mishaps. But if you look around, you are all alive and enjoying this wonderful feast. Still, I can tell from looking on the faces of some of you, you have doubts as to how far you want to go on this river journey of yours. With your permission, I'd like to reflect on something I hope will revitalize you."

Heads nod in approval, so ROJ begins. "I am aware of your job titles from the papers I have been working on and enjoying at the same time. You are all investors, developers. Am I right?"

Once again, nods appear in approval. "Do any of you have any idea where the concept of your job title originates?" ROJ asks.

No nods appear. Just blank faces. "From the very beginning of conquest, warriors were considered the most brave souls there were. They would either scout out territories and report back to their superiors, or they would lead battles to victory. When money came into being, that role took on a whole new perspective in the form of investing. Still, it involved risk-taking, and risk taking involved investments, securities, assets, savings, self-worth, and so forth. That is not unlike in today's society. Obviously, you all have made some type of investment in this golf course community that I have enjoyed working on. And obviously, you all have something to lose if it does not materialize. Am I correct in saying so?"

Without speaking, there are nods everywhere. "The very nature of your title origins represent risk-takers, movers and shakers within your community, people who are not afraid to make improvements for the betterment of others through educated and calculated risks. Do any of you know the origins of the code or creed of your profession?" ROJ asks.

Everyone looks at one another, but no one answers. "You mean to tell me that as investors, not a single one of you know the code or creed of your profession?"

As they continue eating lunch, once again, there are no answers, not even from Ira. "Well, I guess you are expecting me to spell it out for you since I brought it up. As warriors, as investors, as developers, as movers and shakers, the code or creed of your profession is 'What does not kill you makes you stronger.' Have any of you heard that saying before?" ROJ asks.

"Yeah, so what?" asks Aydin.

Michael E. Oppitz

"Don't you know what ROJ is telling us?" Ira interjects. "He's telling us that we should be tougher than we seem. We should have more confidence in each other and ourselves for what we give ourselves credit. We should meet head-on every challenge we encounter with gusto and Exhilaration. When we make a commitment, like with this golf course community, we should be warriors, and act like it any time we encounter difficulties. Difficulties are simply opportunities in disguise."

"So that goes for this river trip as well?" H&M says. "Of course, it does. We all shared a life-changing experience today that could have resulted very differently. Instead, we benefited from it by learning something about ourselves and about how to work together and celebrate life's little surprises," Ira adds. "We are alive and well and enjoying the time of our lives, and it is mostly due to ROJ and his expertise in keeping us safe."

Once again, there is no response. The nods and smiles of everyone's faces say it all.

As they continue to chow down on lunch, Aydin asks, "Where do we go from here, ROJ?"

"There are a few more rapids, but they are pretty much straight through. No cutbacks or anything difficult like that. The last rapid is called Rock Slide. There's a house-size boulder in the middle of the river, and the water goes around it really fast. It's not as difficult as it seems, but the water is faster than anything you have experienced so far. Before exiting Santa Elena, there are two canyons with lots of beauty and some hiking, if you think you want to make time for it," ROJ replies.

191

"How much time are you talking about?" Aydin says again.

"If you all push hard and don't exit the canoes, you can be out of Santa Elena before nightfall. If, however, you want to do some exploring around Smuggler's Cave, that can take a number of hours, we'll have to stay the night in our canoes since there are no beaches or any place where we can get out," ROJ says.

"Can we make that decision after completing the Rock Slide rapid?"

Skye asks.

"Everything is entirely up to you. This your trip. You tell me what you want to do," ROJ replies.

"I think we can make that decision after Rock Slide," Ira interjects.

"Very well. As soon as you are all finished with lunch, we can push off. The next two rapids are class II, bigger than the ones on the Colorado, but straightforward. Just follow me through the notch of each one, and you'll have great time," ROJ adds.

CHAPTER TWENTY-SEVEN

After lunch is over with, ROJ packs up everything. Before pushing off from the eddy, ROJ reminds the group once again to follow him through the notch and do everything he does. The next three rapids are larger than the ones they went through before, but even more fun. No one back paddles anymore. Riding the current ends up being more fun, and of course, splashing goes along with it.

Exiting the the third rapid, ROJ pulls alongside the other canoes. "So how was that?"

"Totally awesome. Too bad we can't go back and do those again!" H&M shouts with joy. "Right on!" Phillip adds.

"You'll just have to come back again sometime. I'll always be here," ROJ says.

"If we do, you will be the only guide for us," Aydin replies. ROJ nods with a smile.

"So what's up with this last rapid—Rock Slide you called it?" Ira asks.

"The river is very narrow with a huge boulder in the middle. The water is very fast going around it, so it deserves a lot of respect. There won't be much time to back paddle, just steering. Bow people, you'll have to reach quickly while your partner steers, otherwise, the current will take you where you don't want to go. I don't want to be scraping anyone off the rocks with one rapid left to go. Telling you how to do this is one thing, actually doing it is another. Watch me and Skye as we go through, and do exactly as we do," ROJ demands.

"No exceptions. Right?" Phillip adds.

"Correct! No exceptions. Stern rowers, bark out instructions constantly. If you are ready, we are getting close as you can tell from the roar of the rapid. Follow me," ROJ says.

ROJ shoots the notch and is immediately swallowed by the fast current. Within seconds, he's steering left with his paddle stuck in the water held tightly up against the canoe. Skye is also reaching left as well. As they round the huge boulder, ROJ yells instructions to Skye to start reaching right. ROJ puts his paddle on the right side turning the canoe rounding the boulder safely and into slower water. They pull ashore where they have a good observation of the others.

Without notice, Aydin and H&M shoot in front and are swallowed through the notch. H&M is reaching as Aydin shouts out instructions, but he is not turning the canoe as fast as ROJ did. Even though the canoe is pointed in the right direction, the fast current is pushing it straight for the boulder. Out of desperation, Aydin begins paddling on the right side, trying to maintain speed so the canoe won't hit the boulder broadside. Instead, H&M's reaching gets them far enough ahead of the boulder that only the very stern hit the boulder, still allowing them enough room to maneuver around it. H&M instinctively begins reaching right, pulling them around the other side while Aydin continues paddling, but on the left, maintaining speed in order to clear the boulder. Finally out of danger, they meet up with ROJ and Skye with a sigh of relief.

Ira and Phillip commit themselves through the notch, and the current immediately swallows them toward the boulder. Both of them have their oars on the left side pulling and steering them around the beast. Without having to bark out a single command, Phillip starts reaching right while Ira also changes sides, steering the canoe safely around. They also meet up with the others.

"That was scary as hell, but what a rush!" H&M rejoices. "I can see how something as simple as that could easily be met with disaster if not done right," Aydin says.

"You are all learning quickly," ROJ replies. "I think you could tackle the lower canyons, if you wanted to."

"I don't know about that," Skye interjects. "You are just a great teacher, ROJ."

"*Amen* to that," Phillip says.

"Well, everyone. What do you want to do? Head out quickly before we lose the sun, or stay on the river and do some exploring tomorrow?" Ira asks.

"What's the camping situation going to be like tonight, if we stay on?" Skye asks.

"You'll be sleeping out in the open in canoes or any flat rock you find, and dinner will be leftovers and cold. Same goes for breakfast, but the wine will be ice cold," ROJ explains.

"Well, one out three isn't too bad," Phillip says immediately. "If you remember what ROJ mentioned to us earlier, we are warriors, movers and shakers. If we don't live up to our titles and take full advantage of this opportunity, then want can be said about ourselves?"

"You know, Phillip, that's probably the wisest thing you have said on this entire trip," Ira states.

Phillip follows Ira's compliment with a smile and a nod. "Agreed, then. ROJ, find us a suitable place to tie up for the night close to each other, and we'll make the most of this tremendous opportunity getting drunk while we figure out why we decided to stay," Skye retorts.

"Follow me, then," ROJ says. They all push off and leisurely make their way through Fern Canyon. The current is calm and hypnotizing. H&M points out the unusual slanted lines in the rock formations as they float by. "Looks like we are floating backward. Strangest thing I have ever witnessed before."

"Strangest and most intoxicating. It's hard to think that we are even here to experience all this. Thanks, Ira, for having the foresight to bring us all along to enjoy this," Skye announces. "It's been my most sincere pleasure to share this with all of you. ROJ is right. This experience is going to make us closer as a team and stronger as individuals," Ira says.

As they pass through Fern Canyon and the optical illusion, ROJ spies a big boulder jetting out into the current providing a safe haven behind it. "Follow me behind that big boulder up ahead. We can tie off and be completely safe for the night."

They each take turns pivoting into the boulder's eddy by back paddling on the right. When they all become secure, ROJ breaks out the wine and says, "This first swig is for Phillip, who came up with the decision to stay. Make it a big one. There's only one more gallon left."

As Phillip takes his most rewarding swig and passes it on, normal chatter and laughter fill the air again. Echoes of laughter are mind absorbing. ROJ breaks out as many leftovers, GORP, and finger food he can find, places them on cooler lids, and passes them around. No one seems to mind that they are roughing it and eating a cold supper, because the company and the location make everything all that more worthwhile.

One gallon disappears quickly from everyone's horrendous appetites and thirst. Halfway through the last gallon, slumber fills the night air. Phillip's snoring doesn't have any effect on the rest. Surprisingly, everyone gets a great night's sleep, especially since sunup comes later than usual with them being between 1,500-foot canyons.

Skye wakes up first, making sure she wakes up everyone else. "Don't remember the last time I slept in my clothes, but being out in open is awesome."

"I don't remember the first time I slept in my clothes," Ira points out, "but I didn't really mind it. Really makes me feel alive."

"After Smuggler's Cave, there's just 2.5 miles left before the take- out. Does anyone want a cold breakfast, or do you want to push on?"

"I say we push on. I need to work off this hangover," Aydin says. "I'm with you, man. Let's get it on," H&M agrees.

As the tie lines are undone, they push off one at a time. An hour around the bend, they come up on a beach area with a naturally well- developed cave on the Mexican side fifty feet up vertical walls. "ROJ, what's this?" Phillip asks demandingly.

"Oh, that's Smuggler's Cave. That's what you stayed all night to see."

"*What!*" Skye shouts in confusion. "How are we supposed to hike that thing? It's straight up!"

"I imagine very carefully," ROJ says trying to keep in his chuckles. While everyone looks at the vertical walls in confusion, not knowing what to think or do, Ira begins laughing under his breath. "We asked for the canoe trip of a lifetime. How many of you are going to look back on this and fondly remember how you slept in a canoe in your clothes under the most serene and beautiful skies imaginable, getting drunk with the most important companions you could ever be blessed to work with, and tell your grandkids all about it with a straight face?" "I hand it to you, ROJ. You are full of surprises, and this one may be one of the most memorable. I put it right up there with nearly being swept over a rock wall and being consumed by an undertow below from which you saved me," Aydin replies.

"With all that we have been through, at least ROJ gave us a working design of our golf course community we can use, and in two nights. I say he gave us our money's worth and more. Many times more, if you ask me," Ira comments with a big smile.

While all gather around, they look at one another in silence while smiles and then laughter begin; With a big group hug, they get in their canoes and push off toward the take-out 2.5 miles downstream. Not much is said, just intermittent chatter, lots of looking around, and contemplating the effects and rewards of an outstanding river trip of a lifetime. The beautiful calm waters between Santa Elena and Mariscal Canyons is just the right mix of comfort and relaxation after spending the last three to four days in a canoe.

Upon beaching the canoes, ROJ walks up to the parking lot where his shuttle has been delivered. Backing the trailer down to the water's edge, he instructs everyone to transfer their belongings from the watertight bags to their suitcases. ROJ is first to put in his supplies so their luggage can be unloaded first. Once the canoes are empty, they help ROJ load the canoes onto the trailer.

The ride back to Lajitas is fairly short and uneventful. Getting out of the truck, each member walks up to ROJ and gives him a hug. Ira, of course, maintains his composure by giving ROJ a hearty handshake and a bill. ROJ puts it in his pocket right away so the others would not see it. "In my dealings as a professional banker, broker, developer and investor, the experience you gave me on the Rio Grande will be endeared for a lifetime. I will always remember you, ROJ."

CHAPTER TWENTY-EIGHT

During one of their weekly conference calls, Marvin Tillman of Computer Solutions says, "Clarence, I have a technical question I'd like to bring to light with one of your technicians. Who would you suggest I talk to about this?"

"What kind of technical question is it so I can recommend the right person to you?" Clarence replies.

"It concerns the location and seating arrangement of one of the computers that I am designing found in your specs. I have a suggestion as to how it can be changed that would work better with the design of other components around it." "Tell you what, the best person to start with is Weyland Reddington, my project manager. He is in charge of all my technicians and line supervisors, and depending on the specific information pertaining to your suggestion, he is the one who can direct you to the exact individual who can answer your question," Clarence says. "Here is his direct phone number in order to avoid going through the switchboard operator."

"Thank you, Clarence. That will save me a lot of time and hassles being able to talk to him directly. Is there a certain time of day that is best to call him with his schedule?" Marvin asks.

"There are no meetings scheduled for the rest of the day, so he can probably be reached anytime," Clarence replies.

"Thank you once again, Clarence. I'll take this matter up with him, and when he reports back to you, perhaps you can give me an update," Marvin says.

"In fact, give me some time, and I'll let him know to expect a call from you."

"You have been a great help, Clarence. Thanks," Marvin says. Later during the day, the phone rings in Weyland Reddington's Office. When he answers, the voice on the other end says, "Hello, Weyland, my name is Marvin Tillman of Computer Solutions."

"Hello, Mr. Tillman. Mr. Patterson informed me that you would be calling. How can I help you?"

"While working with the design specs I received from your boss, I noticed a possible design defect that can be improved in order to compensate further efficiency of the other components around it. Are you capable of handling this situation, or would you recommend I talk to someone else who is closer to the construction of the housing and knows where and how all the components are to be situated all together?" Mr. Tillman asks.

"If you allow me some time, I will be glad to look into it and get back with you. Would that be agreeable?" Weyland asks.

"Yes, of course. I would, however, like to hear back from you as soon as possible in order to proceed with the installation of my computer components."

"I understand time is of the utmost importance here. I'll look into it right away and have Mr. Patterson contact you immediately once he gets my report," Weyland replies.

Weyland walks down to the production area and seeks out the line supervisor in charge of the construction of the computer component housing. It takes a while for Weyland to locate the supervisor because he's busy walking the production area, constantly answering questions or concerns from the production employees. Each employee has a specific area within the housing hull, so they all have to work in unison in order for the construction to operate smoothly. Weyland finally spots the supervisor inspecting someone's assembly. "Lester, I'm glad I found you. I'm also glad to see you constantly inspecting the constructing of these housing components. Can't tell you how important that is, and I can tell you take a lot of pride in your work."

"How can you help you, Mr. Reddington?"

"Lester, I need to look at the blueprints with you to determine another option for redesigning a specific seating arrangement for one of the computer components so it will be more compatible with the other computer components that will be situated around it," Weyland exclaims.

"Are you referring to this seating arrangement located right here on the blueprints?" Lester Jones asks.

"Why, yes. How did you know?" Weyland asks, astonished. "I noticed that design flaw more than a week ago and placed my suggestion about it in the suggestion box. I have been waiting to get feedback from it," Lester replies.

Weyland just stands there and remains speechless for what seems like a minute and finally says, "You mean to tell me, Lester, that you already observed this design flaw and took it upon yourself to suggest correcting it all on your own?" Weyland says surprisingly.

"Yes, sir. I even made notation on the blueprint where a more suitable location would be," Lester replies.

"Do you have a few minutes to go over your suggestion with me right now?" Weyland asks.

"Yes, sir. Let's do it."

Lester fishes out his suggestion from the box along with the blueprint and shows his modification ideas to Weyland.

"Outstanding. You recognized this before anyone else, and I failed in my responsibility to check this suggestion box regularly in order to respond back to you. You have proven to me, Lester, the ultimate importance that the flow of communication has in all levels within an organization, and I am totally grateful to you. I have learned something today, and I have you to thank for that. I'm going to report this to Mr. Patterson so he can pass it on to Computer Solutions. You can be proud that you have been instrumental in solving a simple design problem that could have escalated."

"Thanks, Mr. Reddington. I appreciate that very much," Lester replies.

"I want to reward you with a big bonus, and I know Mr. Patterson will accept my proposal in doing so. You can expect to see it in your next paycheck," Weyland says, grabbing Lester's hand. "You truly have an angel looking after you when I gave you that second chance. It's taken time, but I am a true believer now."

Lester looks perplexed, not knowing what was just said, but he nods and smiles just the same.

CHAPTER TWENTY-NINE

Judd Henson walks into work with his usual cup of black coffee and a huge blueberry muffin. The regional Park Service office is made with all-natural materials to blend in with the local stucco decor of the southwest. Beautiful Southwest tapestries decorate the walls of the entryway with a glass case of some of the local artistry, containing silverwork, jewelry, and beadwork. His office is in the corner, out of the way of everyone else's, with a big wooden door handcrafted with a bear on the front. His big wooden desk was also handcrafted by a local builder. Pictures of canyons, sunsets, and rivers add to the wall decor along with his handmade shelves. Rustling through papers is more of a necessary evil than anything else. Judd's favorite things to look forward to during his workday is to travel somewhere on assignment where he knows he can do the most good.

Judd's secretary, Madeline, comes over the phone speaker and says, "Do you know a Mr Clyde Harrison from Indianapolis, Indiana?"

Michael E. Oppitz

"No. Doesn't ring a bell. Did he say what he wants?" Judd replies. "Something about the estate of a Terrence Jasper." "Yes, it does ring a bell now. Put him through, please."

"Hello. This is Judd Henson, regional Park Service officer." "Hello, Mr. Henson. Please allow me to introduce myself. My name is Clyde Harrison, attorney-at-law, and I represent the late Terrence Jasper along with his wife, Eleanor, and son, Robbie. Are you familiar with those names?" "Yes, sir, I am."

"Excellent. When I received word that Terrence Jasper met his demise on the Rio Grande, you probably had some idea how I felt about losing a well-respected community member, international professional, and friend," Mr. Harrison says.

"Yes, I do, and I know it makes it even more difficult to hear that he was a good friend as well," Judd replies.

"Yes, it does, and thank you. Now, to the reason for my calling. Are you aware of the whereabouts of Robbie Jasper since I have been informed that he left the hospital as your responsibility?"

"I was asked in the utmost confidence not to speak of Robbie or his whereabouts," Judd says sternly.

"I see. That means, however, that you are aware of his whereabouts, whether or not you are so inclined to speak of it," Mr. Harrison replies sharply.

"Yes. I guess that is what it means. Would you be so kind as to tell me what this is about?" Judd asks.

206

"If there is any remote possibility of finding Robbie, I guess I have no choice. I was charged with the responsibility of being executor of the Jasper Estate, and I need to speak with Robbie about the assets and holdings that have been placed in his name. I also need to know what Robbie's intentions are regarding the Jasper Estate. Does that help?" Mr. Harrison explains.

"Yes, Mr. Harrison. That helps a lot. I will contact Robbie and get back with you as to his interests and intentions. Please leave your contact information and any documents he needs in reference to the estate with my secretary. By the way, how did you know to contact me?" Judd asks.

"Robbie's girlfriend was told where he and his family were vacationing, and the regional Park Service office was just a commonsense place to begin my search. In fact, she was the only one who seemed to know where Robbie and his family were going," Mr. Harrison replies.

"As soon as I have something to share with you, I will contact you. Don't know how long it will take, though," Judd says.

"Not too long, I hope. I look forward to hearing back from you. Thank you for your help," Mr. Harrison says before hanging up.

"Madeline, I'm going to be gone for a while to Big Bend. Don't know how long I will be, but I will stay in constant touch with you," Judd says as he scurries around his office, gathering papers and supplies for a long drive to southwest Texas. "I'm going home to pack, then I'm off."

"Drive safely, and take care," Madeline says as Judd rushes out his office and through the entrance doors.

After a five-hour drive through southwest Texas, he finally reaches the city limits of Lajitas. He makes his way through town, past the downtown businesses, and down toward the Rio Grande where the river trip vendors are located. Finding his usual parking spot away from the tourists in a secluded corner of the parking area, he walks past all the vendors, down to the river and makes the right turn heading upriver. The mile hike to ST's camp seems longer every time. Going around the bend, he spots the camp where FAM and DBoR are gathering firewood for what appears to be a week's supply. "Look what the filthy cat drug in," FAM says in her usual 'sultry' self.

"I'm in no mood for your insults today, FAM. Where's ST?" Judd demands.

"Hey, ST. Get your buns out here. Judd face wants a word with you!" FAM hollers.

"Judd. What does that dead weight want now?" ST answers. "Hey, stop calling me names until you know why I'm here. Is Robbie about?"

"You mean, ROJ? He's on a three- to-four-day river trip," ST replies. "Who's ROJ?" Judd asks bewildered.

"That's your so-called Robbie. That's the name he has adopted, so when you're in our neck of the woods, that's the name he prefers. Got it?" ST says.

"Got it. When did … ROJ leave?"

"About four days ago. Just waiting for him to arrive with the shuttle and his party. He should be walking around the bend in a day or two, or whenever he gets here," ST casually says.

"Boy, you are a bunch of help today. I guess I'll have to wait for him in town. At least Rachael will know when he'll be back. Good day to you all," Judd says scoldingly as he turns around and leaves around the bend. Reaching Rachael's building, Judd enters and says, "Good day to you, Rachael. How is life treating you?"

"Not bad. Not bad at all. What can I do you for, Judd?" "Will you be kind enough to keep me informed when ROJ and his party get back?" Judd asks.

"Sure. I heard that his party should be landing sometime today or tomorrow. When he checks in, do you want me to let you know right away?" Rachael says.

"That sounds super. Just find me around town, and thanks," Judd replies.

The next morning, a very attractive young blonde girl is at the Southwest Texas Outfitter's building asking questions pertaining to Robbie Jasper. Christine is wearing her usual baggy clothes, but her hiking shorts still adorn her shapely curves. Instead of her usual Converse tennis shoes, she has sported thongs which were a bad choice because the dust completely conceals the natural blue color. Even though most river vendors don't keep track of the river rats, Alexandria, the receptionist, instructs her to go over to Rachael's building. Rachel's building is mostly an information center for tourists and those who don't know what they are doing. Her shack is small probably measuring twelve by fifteen. There are pictures of canoeists and white water all over the walls. The information desk has a window display with the names of all of the river trip vendors listed. Rachel is a very attractive young woman in her early 20s with long thick dark hair. Her natural tan accentuates her beautiful features. When the young guides have time on their hands, they are spotted venturing in and out of her little shack. As she walks in, she introduces herself. "Hello, my name is Christine, and I am inquiring about the whereabouts of Robbie Jasper. I know he and his family went on a river trip from here."

"Can you be a little more specific about any information that would help me place that name," Rachael asks.

"He and his family contracted a river guide down the Rio Grande. It was met with disaster, and his parents were never seen again," Christine explains almost in tears.

"Oh yeah, I remember. In fact, ST from upriver was hired by the Park Service to go find them. Found only the boy and took him to the hospital. In fact, the Park Service officer who took Robbie to the hospital, along with ST, the guide, is here in town. You probably want to talk to him. He knows more than anyone about the incident. His name is Judd Henson," Rachael replies.

"How do I find him?"

"He's wearing his Park Service uniform and will be back here inquiring about a few things tomorrow. In case I see him before you do, can I have him contact you?" Rachael asks.

"I don't know where I will be staying. Just got to town. If you recommend a place, I can be contacted there," Christine says.

"Sure. All the hotels along here are full of tourists, but the Lajitas House Hotel outside of town probably has room. Tell you what. I'll call ahead so they will know you are coming. I'll let you know when I see Judd. Will that help?" Rachael

"You've been more help than I could possibly imagine. Thank you very much," Christine says as she takes the hotel information from Rachael and leaves.

She walks over to her car and takes a slow drive through downtown. Much of it looks like it came right out of an old west movie. "Quaint," she whispers to herself. A left turn at the end of town and another left at the curse puts her on the edge of town and in front of her hotel. It, too, resembles those building of downtown and truly has that old west feeling about it. As she checks in, it's nice to see the old fashion receptionist desk polished to a shine in mahogany wood, an old fashion reading lamp in the corner providing the only illumination, and an manual money register.

"Hello," Christine delightfully says. "My name is Christine, and Rachel called to let you know I was on my way."

"Oh yes. Very professional and helpful that dear is," the middle aged receptionist replies. "I have you in room 218, a very nice single bed room overlooking downtown. I hope you enjoy your stay."

"I know I will, but I'm not here by choice. Trying to find my boyfriend. Anyways, thank you very much." Christine makes her way to her room, gets settled in, then lays down on the bed with tears beginning to form in her eyes.

The next morning, Judd Henson shows up like he said inquiring about Robbie's party. "Any news yet about Robbie's party landing?" Judd asks.

"No, not yet. Hey, there a pretty young blonde looking for Robbie. Know anything about that?" Rachael inquires.

"No. Is it of any importance?"

"I don't know. I'm leaving that up to you. I told her I would call her when I see you so the two of you can hash it out," Rachael says.

"Why leave it up to me?"

"Because you were the last person responsible for Robbie when he arrived back in town. Now deal with it!" Rachael exclaimed harshly.

"Very well. Call and let her know to meet me at the restaurant," Judd says.

"Done. Will be glad to get this over with," Rachael replies. "You and me both," Judd says.

At 9:00 am, Christine receives a phone call from Rachel. "Hey Christine, are you awake, yet?"

"I am now. What's up?"

"That Park Service guy I told you about? Well, he's over at the downtown restaurant waiting for you. Can't miss him since he's wearing his uniform. He's waiting for you."

"Thanks, Rachel. Don't know what I'd do without you being in a town I know nothing about."

Judd makes his way to the restaurant, sits down in a booth facing the door, and orders his black coffee with a blueberry muffin. Christine throws on her clothes as quickly as possible, brushes her hair as she runs out the door, and towards the restaurant. It's only a few minutes job from her Hotel. Ten minutes later, a pretty young blonde, just as Rachael described her, walks through the front door. Upon seeing his uniform, she makes a beeline straight toward him. "Hello, my name is Christine, and I'm inquiring about Robbie Jasper. I was told you had the most reliable information to share."

"Hello, Christine, my name is Judd Henson, regional Park Service officer. And yes, I do know something about Robbie. Please sit down so we can discuss our interests in him. By the way, how do you know Robbie?"

"I've known Robbie all his life. We have been best friends forever, and just before he left for his family vacation, I became his girlfriend,"

Christine says with a heavy heart.

"I see. And how did you know to find him here?" Judd asks.

"I was the only person he told where he and his family were going. I found out about Robbie and his accident through the media. I couldn't wait any longer. I had to do something. Before he left, I told him if he didn't come back to me, I'd find him," Christine now says with tears in her eyes.

"I think it's wonderful to have someone so devoted as you to go after someone you lost regardless of the circumstances. That shows a special bond between the two of you and tremendous character on your part," Judd says. "When he gets back from his river trip, I will visit with him and get back with you. I made arrangements with Clyde Harrison, executor of the Jasper Estate, to have copies of all paperwork, documents, bank accounts, holdings, and assets pertaining to the Jasper Estate to be overnighted to my office. Instead of him coming here, he has trusted me to present to Robbie everything he needs to know about his father's worth and decide what he wants to do next. But you have to promise me something."

"Yes. What's that?" Christine asks.

"Stay at your hotel. Please don't pursue Robbie. He experienced a very traumatic experience with losing his parents. He doesn't need you barging into his life all of a sudden upsetting his new and different life. Stay here until I come get you. Can you do that?" Judd asks.

"Yeah, I guess. I just feel so powerless coming all this way. But now that I'm here, I can wait a few more days. I'll do as you ask. Promise," Christine says.

"Good. I hope so, for his sake. I'll be in touch soon. I promise. I'm driving to my office today and will return by tomorrow. When I have everything I need, we'll decide where to go from there," Judd says.

CHAPTER THIRTY

Judd drives all the way back to his office five hours away, stays the night, and receives the package from Clyde Harrison the next morning just before noon. He then drives back to Lajitas, arriving at 5:00 p.m. Upon entering town, he drives over to the Lajitas House Hotel and finds Christine. "Christine, I received all the assets associated with the Jasper Estate, and it has not been opened. On my way back to Lajitas to see you, I decided on what would be the best course of action concerning Robbie and his father's estate."

"Are you going to present the contents of that packet to Robbie and have him tell you what he wants to do?" Christine asks.

"No, I'm not. You are."

"Me. Why me?" Christine asks in bewilderment.

"You know Robbie better than anyone in this world. I want you to spend the evening going through everything in that packet, then I want you to decide how you are going to present to him all that information after you see how he has changed. Only you can make a decision like that. I'm not qualified. You are, and I know you will find the best way to tell Robbie about his father's financial worth and what he wants to do about it. So please, think about this hard. I will pick you up at the hotel around eleven a.m. after you've had a chance to eat breakfast," Judd says.

"OK, Mr. Henson, I'll be ready, but scared."

"I know you'll be fine. See you tomorrow, kid," Judd says as he walks out the door.

Looking at the bulging manilla packet of information given to her by Judd, tears begin to well up in her eyes. "No you don't. Not again. You have important business to attend to, and this is no time to get emotional again," she says to herself under her breath.

Christine takes the stuffed packet of information back to her hotel room, opens it, and scatters its contents all over the bed. Trying to put all the information into some type of organized fie system winds up being a monumental task. Since Mr. Jasper traveled all over the world with his profession, there are investment accounts from all over the world. There are accounts from Switzerland, Thailand, Germany, Helsinki, and even Hong Kong. Christine found a holding account in Robbie's name that would be available to him once he reaches the age of twenty- one. The Jasper Estate alone contains documents including the deed for the property, which is substantial just by itself, and the mansion, which is even more substantial. There are multiple checking accounts in Mr. Jasper's name, his wife's name, and the holding account for Robbie when he reaches twenty-one. There are also multiple savings accounts, CDs, T-bills and other local investments. Clyde Harrison did a great job allocating a numerical value to everything that didn't already have one so the court system would approve its validity more rapidly.

By the time she organizes everything in its proper category, the total sum of Mr. Jasper's financial worth exceeds 12.5 million dollars. When Christine finally has a total sum, her jaw drops, and she just stands there in total awe, not knowing what to think or how to present this onslaught of information to Robbie. How would he react? What would he do with all this? These thoughts perplex her to point where she is getting a headache. She has to come up with some type of game plan, and it would take her most of the night to go over all the scenarios of how Robbie would react. Sleeping on it would be the best course of action for now. She puts all the information back in the packet, gets ready for bed and tries to get some sleep. Easier said than done. It is 3:00 a.m. before she finally doses off.

Waking up at 9:30 a.m., refreshed, taking a shower and getting dressed would hopefully give her the insight she needs to deal with the task of confronting Robbie today. It didn't help. She still feels confused and has no game plan. "I need something to eat and a big cup of coffee to get my mind straight," Christine says to herself. "Wait a minute, I don't drink coffee. Well, maybe today is a good time to begin."

The short walk to the restaurant still leaves her mind clouded. After consuming a big bowl of oatmeal with raisins and brown sugar, toast and jelly, and three eggs over easy, and a big cup of coffee that is hard to stomach because it is her first time tasting coffee, she slowly walks back to her hotel room. While the caffeine from the coffee kicks in and she begins to fidget,

11:00 a.m. could not come fast enough. Finally, Judd Henson knocks on her door. Christine opens it.

"Hey, kid, you ready to go and get this over with?" Judd asks.

"I don't know if I'm ready, but I do want to see Robbie again, and, yes, get this over with."

They both get in Judd's jeep and head over to where the river trip vendors are located. Judd parks in his usual parking space in the corner of the lot away from every other vehicle. When they get out, Judd and Christine walk over toward the vendors, and Judd can tell Christine is nervous. "Christine, you don't have to be so nervous. I know you will do just fine once you see Robbie."

"That's only part of it. I had a big cup of coffee this morning, and I don't drink coffee," Christine says, fidgeting. "Yeah, if you're not used to the effects caffeine has on your system, you picked a poor time to start drinking coffee. Once adrenaline takes over, you won't feel anything else. Trust me.

Now just try to relax and maintain an open mind," Judd advises. When they reach the vendors, Judd turns to Christine, softly grabs her wrist and looking her straight into her eyes says, "Now Christine, Iam going the camp where Robbie lives. I will tell him the situation, or at least as much as he will permit me, and return with him. Please prepare yourself."

"Prepare myself? How? For what?"

"Robbie probably has changed quite a bit since you last saw him. I just want you to have an open mind and don't jump to any conclusions. Can you do that?" Judd asks.

"Yes, I will do my very best," Christine replies rather subdued.

"Hang in there, Christine. Now it's a mile walk to his camp. After I inform him as to what is going on, it's a mile walk back here. Find a comfortable place to sit, and I'll be back in a little while. Please be patient," Judd says as he walks down toward the river and disappears around the bend.

Waiting for the inevitable is probably the most difficult thing Christine has done in her life. After everything she has gone through finding Robbie's whereabouts and finally being here waiting to see him again after the accident, waiting is excruciating. If she's not pacing in her mind as to what will happen, the coffee's caffeine kicks in, and she begins fidgeting. "How does Judd think I'm going to be OK, waiting like this? This is horrible. I can't stand it any longer."

Just as she gets up to start walking around in order to occupy her mind, she sees Judd return around the bend on the river. He does not come toward her, but rather gives her a head nod and walks out of sight.

When she looks back down toward the river, she doesn't recognize the person walking up the bank. He is taller than six foot two inches and has long dark hair hanging down to his shoulders, a neatly trimmed mustache and beard, and huge chest that completely fills out the T-shirt he's wearing along with ripped muscles. The khaki shorts he's wearing sports a thin waist with well-developed thigh and calf muscles. He looks more like a male model than anything else. Finally, her mind kicks in, and Christine realizes that this hunk of a young man must be Robbie. She walks over toward him, slowly, with the packet of information. He recognizes her before her mind realizes it is truly Robbie. His huge approving smile gives him away, and she runs toward him.

She doesn't even slow down, and while he's able to catch her in his huge arms, she nearly knocks him down.

She holds him and cries uncontrollably. "Robbie, I finally found you. I told you I would. I'm never letting you go. I told you I would find you, and I have," Christine says without unleashing her grip on him. "I'm never letting you go again." She holds him tightly without relinquishing her grasp.

After what seemed like half an hour, Robbie replies. "I knew you would find me. My life was over with my parents gone, but I knew you would find me. I'm so glad you did.

You have always been in my thoughts. You," he says holding back tears of joy.

Finally, after ten minutes or more, she loosens her grasp on him long enough to plant a big kiss on him. "That's the kiss I remember. Now I know it is you. Please take me some place where we can talk. I want to know everything about you and your new life you have carved out for yourself," Christine says while still crying.

"Christine, my darling. I have missed you so much, but I couldn't return to my normal life because nothing was normal anymore. My perspective on what happened changed me forever, and there was no way I could explain that to you back in your life. You had to see me for who I am now. This is the only way I can show you who I am now and why. You may or may not approve, but I am hoping you will. Your approval is very important to me, but I have to be honest to you and also with my own heart when I say this is my life now. There is no returning with you and trying to begin where we left off. Honestly,

I don't think I would know how after what I have been through. I sincerely hope you are able to grasp what I am trying to say to you," Robbie pleads.

"It would help if you tell me what you are doing now that has transformed you so much," Christine says sniffling.

"The brave soul who braved the Rio Grande to find me and saved my life is a river rat. Someone who lives on the river and guides tourists down the Rio Grande River. He is one of the bravest and most modest persons I have ever met. When I asked to be introduced to him where he lives, I instantly found his surroundings and his line of work to the most relaxing, peaceful and nonstressed environment I have ever experienced. That's when I knew right then and there I wanted to be a river rat. I don't know how else to explain it. I finally found my calling from the most exaggerated and horrific circumstances. This is my life now, and I love it. I love it very much. It's me," Robbie says calmly.

"I totally respect you, Robbie, and what you have told me. I too would like to meet this brave person who snatched you from the river and see firsthand the life of a river rat," Christine says, gathering herself.

"If you are truly interested in seeing my new life, I would be pleased to show you. Are you ready?" Robbie asks.

"Yes. I want to see for myself. I'm ready to follow you into another world and see what has transformed the man I love," Christine says, giving Robbie another kiss. "Let's go. I'm ready."

Robbie takes hold of Christine's hand and leads her down toward the river, turns right, and continues walking the mile toward his camp. The entire mile walk, she notices how soft but firm his hand is. They maintain their grasp the whole time. Along the way, she notices the beauty of the river, its calm flow, and the tranquility it brings staring at it. Birds and bird songs are everywhere. Beautiful rock formations jet out of the ground everywhere with scrub brush and cacti complementing the landscape. There is no section of land that is the same. All the while they continue their walk along the river bank, she constantly holds his grip tight. There is nothing that will separate them again.

After following a slight bend in the river, there is a small group of used tents of different colors decorated with very used lawn chairs some with missing straps. A smoldering fire is attended by a woman and a guy who looks like he has been working out. He is quite muscular, but not as big as her Robbie. The woman is the first to notice them, she stands up and immediately says, "ROJ, you piece of shit. Where have you been? ST has been looking for you. Wants someone to take a family on a short trip through the Colorado," FAM says in her usual raspy voice.

"Wow, that's one way to be greeted, and who is ROJ?" Christine says. "That's my name. It was given to me by the gentleman who saved my life. If you think about it, Christine, it's my initials. I like it very much," ROJ says.

"Hmmm. ROJ. I guess I can get used to it. So who is the pleasant woman who just greeted us?"

"That's FAM. She likes to insult everyone for no reason at all. Just keep your distance, and don't stare at her unless you want more of the same. That other guy is DboR. He's the muscle of our group but isn't very sharp. He pretty much minds his own business. I don't see Hooty anywhere. He must

222

be off hunting for food. Please follow me, and I'll introduce you to ST, the guy who saved me," ROJ explains.

Christine follows ROJ around the pathetic looking tents toward another used tent off by itself. "ST, please come out. I want to introduce you to someone very special," ROJ shouts. "I thought I was the only one who is special around here," ST yells jokingly. As a figure emerges from the tent, Christine spies a thin resemblance of a man with long dirty blond hair that hangs down his back, a bushy and dirty blond mustache that rustles with every breath, and blue jean shorts supported by thin but muscular legs. "OK, you got me out of my slumber, ROJ. This had better be good."

"Christine, please meet ST, the leader of our camp and the gentleman who saved my life," ROJ announces.

Immediately, Christine walks over to ST and gives him a big hug. After releasing him, she says, "I don't think I have ever been this affectionate before. I don't know what got into me."

"That's OK. Remind me to save his life more often," ST says with a big smile on his face that finally exposes his teeth through his bushy mustache.

"I just want to show my appreciation for saving the life of the man I love," Christine says with a slightly bowed head.

"ROJ is definitely one of a kind, and a natural river rat. Don't know what I'd do without him anymore. He is truly family," ST says with gratitude in his voice.

"Family. That's something I'd like to know what has become so important in his new life and how it has changed him so. I'm not saying I don't like it.

It's very new for me to comprehend, and I'd like the opportunity to find out firsthand," Christine says firmly.

"ROJ, this is your court, now," ST says.

"Christine, you are the most important person in my life right now, and I would love to show you my new life," ROJ says.

"Before we begin, would you please excuse me? I need to run back to town and take care of a few arrangements, then I'll be right back. Is that OK?" Christine asks.

"Sure, take all the time you need," ROJ replies.

"No need. Just a little while, then I'll come right back. Promise."

Christine heads back to town along the riverbank with packet in hand. When she reaches town, she immediately heads toward the vendor that Rachael operates. "Hi, Rachael, my name is Christine. Do you remember me?"

"Yes, of course I do. How can I be of service to you?" "Very well- spoken. I am in need of a bank where I can make a wire transfer of funds. Can you recommend any bank to me?" asks Christine.

"Sure. The West Texas State Bank is very reliable. They're in town just down the street. Shall I call to let them know you are coming?"

"You are the best, Rachael. Thank you," Christine says.

Christine walks down the street to the bank, walks through the door, and goes directly to the Vice President's office. To the annoyance of the receptionist in front, she opens the door and announces herself. "Hello, I would like to make a long-distance phone call and transfer a substantial amount of funds to your bank. Can you help me?"

"The receptionist is equipped to handle all new accounts and direct them to the appropriate individual to accommodate your requests," he says.

"Excuse me, I am wanting to make a long-distance phone call in order to transfer hundreds of thousands—if not millions—of dollars to an account to this bank. I don't want to waste my time talking to a receptionist. I want to talk to someone who can make things happen right now. Do you understand?" Christine demands.

"Uh, yes. I guess I do understand. Please use my phone," the VP says. Christine dials the phone number listed for Clyde Harrison. After multiple rings, he finally answers. "Hello, this is Mr. Harrison, attorney-at-law."

"Hello, Mr. Harrison. My name is Christine, and Judd Henson trusted me with the packet of information concerning the Jasper Estate. Did you receive a phone call from him concerning this? Do you recall the information you overnighted to him?"

"Yes, Christine. I do. How can I help you?" Mr. Harrison replies. "I am the Chief Financial Officer for Robbie Jasper and the Jasper Estate since Judd Henson trusted me with the information. I am calling you from the West Texas State Bank in Lajitas, Texas, and I want you to consolidate the checking and savings accounts in the Jaspers' names and place them into a checking account in Robbie's name, and I want you to do that right now," Christine demands.

"Since Judd Henson already called me approving you as holder of Robbie's financial information, I will be glad to accommodate your request. I just need to speak to a bank official to verify your location and intent," Mr. Harrison replies.

"That's fine. I will put you on the phone with Mr. Tyler Crompton, Vice President of the bank. He will take care of the details. Will that be satisfactory?" Christine asks.

"Yes, Christine. That will be fine. Please put him on the phone," Mr. Harrison says.

It doesn't take long for the transaction to take place, and Mr. Harrison transfers 1.5 million dollars to a checking account in Robbie's name. As Mr. Crompton looks at the account information, he says, "Christine, this may seem very peculiar to you, but there is already an account in Robbie's name. A gentleman stopped by just a few days ago to make a deposit and left this envelope. He was very direct with his instructions that no one, except Robbie, could open it. Since you have made an additional deposit into his existing account, I can give this to you as long as you sign for it and take responsibility for it. Please have Robbie come by the bank to verify the account information and establish his signature card."

Christine just stands there staring at the envelope, not knowing what to say or do.

"Christine, are you all right? Can I get you anything?" Mr. Crompton says.

After an entire minute, she begins blinking again, she thanks Mr. Crompton for his help, and slowly walks out the door, still appearing to be stunned. "Who could possibly be making a deposit in Robbie's name? No one knows he's here. Who does he know who would be so secretive?" she is thinking to herself. Christine is so perplexed. Her confusion starts changing to excitement. She wants to know who would want to make a deposit to Robbie. Now she can't wait.

With this important information that only she knows, it lifts her spirit and confidence toward her relationship and also toward her position in the river rats. She walks down toward the river, turns right and walks the mile to ROJ's camp. After a while, she finally arrives back at camp. "Glad you finally made it back. Didn't know what you had planned or if you would even come back," ROJ says.

"He who has little faith," says Christine. "ROJ, would you do me a tremendous favor?"

"Sure, Christine, just name it."

"Would you go to town with me to run some errands?"

"Errands? What kind of errands? Don't we need to ask everyone else what they need and make a list? I don't understand," ROJ says perplexed at her idea.

"Please trust me, ROJ. There's no need asking what everyone else needs. I already have that covered. I just need you. Can you do that for me?" Christine asks.

"I don't know what you are up to, but, OK. I'll trust you. You came all this way to find me, and I will trust you completely. This is really becoming interesting," ROJ says enthusiastically.

"Who's that other guy? Is that Hooty you were talking about?" "Yes, that's Hooty."

"Please introduce me to him."

"Christine, meet Hooty. Hooty, meet Christine, my girlfriend." "That was simple enough, but effective.

"Hey, Hooty, would you and DBoR please assemble a huge pile of wood for the biggest bonfire you have ever seen.

When ROJ and I get back, you can light it. Would you do that, please?" Christine asks.

"I don't know what you have planned, but OK. It'll be done," Hooty replies.

The two start walking, and it's not long before they reach town. Christine says, "ROJ, please follow me, and do as I say. That's all you have to do."

"I think I can manage that," ROJ replies.

They walk over to the outfitters store. As soon as they enter, a kind and helpful saleswoman approaches them. "Hello, my name is Kathleen. How can I help you?"

"Hello, Kathleen. My name is Christine, Chief Financial Officer of the river rats, and this is ROJ. I have a list of items I would like you to fill and place them in four brand-new ABS plastic Tejas canoes and place everything on the river bank. Before I walk over to the bank to have a cashier's check made out for these items on my list, please give me an exact total dollar amount," Christine says.

"Sure thing. Please give me a moment, and I'll have a dollar amount ready for you."

Kathleen comes back a few minutes later with a dollar amount at the bottom of the list.

"Will you please write that down for me while you work on the list?" Christine asks.

Christine and ROJ leave the store and head over to the West Texas State Bank. As they enter through the main double doors, they approach the counter. "Excuse me. I was just in here not long ago with Mr. Crompton. ROJ would like to establish his signature card, and I would like to be put on the account as well."

"Please excuse me for just a moment while I confirm your account with Mr. Crompton."

She comes back a moment later with the paperwork for ROJ's account and two signature cards. "Christine, what's this all about? Who's account are we signing for?" ROJ asks. "Yours, silly. I had your parent's checking and savings accounts consolidated into one account in your name. All you have to do is sign for your account to become active, and I will handle everything else. Does that seem simple enough?" Christine replies.

"Yeah, I guess so. You mean I have money?"

"Of course, you have money. You don't have to worry about ever using it because I will take care of all that for you when we decide together how and when to use it," Christine says.

Michael E. Oppitz

"Well, all right then. As long as you take care of it. I don't even want to think about it. I love my life just the way it is," ROJ says.

"I know you do, and I'm glad to do this for you. You are the reason I'm here, and you're the reason why I am going to stay."

"You're going to stay?"

"Of course, I'm going to stay. You are the love of my life," Christine says trying to hold back tears.

ROJ gives her a big hug and a kiss right in the middle of the bank lobby while everyone is staring. When their embrace is finished, the silence converts back to normal bank chatter. "Before we leave, please make out a cashier's check to Rio Grande Outfitters in this amount," Christine asks.

While the cashier is making out the cashier's check, Christine asks ROJ, "Don't you want to know how much money there is in your account?"

"No, and don't care. You said you want to take of that stuff, so . . . take care of it."

Christine responds with a big smile on her face and kisses ROJ. No words are necessary. "Here you go, miss. You're all ready," the cashier says.

"Thank you very much. You may be seeing a lot of me. Please remember that I'm the Chief Financial Officer of him and the river rats," Christine says as they turn around and leave.

When they get outside the bank, Christine says, "Before we go any farther, Mr. Crompton from the bank gave me this envelope to give to you. I don't know anything about it except it is in your name. Do you want to open it now or later?"

"Since it was entrusted to you to give to me, I'll open it now," ROJ says. As he opens the envelope, ROJ pulls out a letter. It reads:

Dear ROJ,

I hope this letter finds you healthy and safe. I want to begin by saying thank you for a very exciting and memorable journey that will give all of us memories that will last a lifetime. Your gourmet cooking was also totally awesome (I actually gained 5 pounds). The designs and specs you created for my group proved to be some of the best I have ever seen. The golf course designer and architect who stamped his seal of approval on the professional recreations of your designs also agreed.

Your expertly created designs and specs saved us three to six months, or more, of hassles and delays if we hired a professional company to do it for us. Upon submitting your designs to the financial institution that is financing our investment, it was approved within a week, saving us another three months if we had to go through the normal banking system.

In all, you saved us six to nine months of hassles and delays which would have been money lost because of time. Once everything was approved, our marketing team got to work. By the time we started breaking ground for our golf course community, eighty percent of all lots were already sold. The response was so overwhelming, we had to hire extra phone operators to handle the response.

The normal commission for hiring a professional company to do what you did which would have taken six to nine months, and that's a conservative estimate, is ten percent of the total investment. You saved us that amount of time so construction could start as soon as possible, allowing us to get ahead of the game. There is nothing normal about you. In fact, I would consider you a genius. Therefore, my entire group of investors, whom you met on the river, agreed with the increased commission that has already been deposited into an account in your name. It was a tremendous pleasure meeting you, volunteering to work for us, feeding us some of the most delicious food we have ever tasted, and saving us a world of time and money. You also saved my life, if you remember. Please enjoy your commission, and by the way, Tyler Clemens sends his fondest regards.

Yours Very Sincerely,

Ira Dresden,
President & CEO and your friend
Investment Solutions

CHAPTER THIRTY-ONE

A s ROJ pulls out the deposit receipt, the amount reads "7.5 million dollars."

Christine has to sit down, and her face starts turning white. "Christine, are you all right? Can I get you anything?" ROJ says immediately.

"I'm fine. Just need a moment. I'm not going to ask you where that came from or what you did to deserve that because I know you are capable of doing anything you put your mind to. Everything about you, ROJ, since I finally got you back in my life again, is mysterious. But, that's what is so appealing to me. Everything you have become is a result of being bottled up by controlling parents. The life you have chosen has allowed you to flourish in the most unpredictable ways. I think it's awesome," Christine says.

As they walk back to the outfitters, ROJ says, "You are something else, Christine. I have no idea how much my father is worth or how much you put in my bank account. Frankly, I don't want to know. That life is no longer important to me, but I'm so glad you are in life again. Can't tell you how much I have missed you and didn't know how I could tell you. I am so blessed you did that for me and by finding me. Just like you said, I know I can trust you with anything including my life," ROJ says with a slight sniffle in his voice.

"The good times are just beginning. Trust me," Christine replies with a smirk on her face.

Upon entering the outfitters, Kathleen greets them and says, "We're almost finished with your list. Would like to inspect what we have assembled so far?"

"You two take care of things. I'm going to walk down by the canoes," ROJ says.

"Kathleen, I am chief financial officer of the river rats, and you will be seeing a lot more of me. Here is the cashier's check for the amount. How much longer?"

"My guys will finish in just a few moments. After you inspect everything that has been loaded in your canoes, let me know if you have any questions. Otherwise, I look forward to seeing you again sometime in the near future," Kathleen says. "Thank you very much," Christine says as she exits the store and heads down to the river.

ROJ is already with the canoes when Christine arrives. "Wow, that is a lot of stuff. What are your plans for it all?"

"You'll see ROJ, but I think you will be pleased. Let's head back to camp," Christine says.

They tie up the canoes and head back to camp. Fighting against the current takes twice as long, but they manage to arrive no more than twenty minutes later. "Wow, that was a workout," Christine says.

After beaching the canoes and walking to camp, Christine asks ROJ, "Would you please ask everyone to assemble by the wood pile. I would like to explain the loaded canoes and what they are for"

ROJ walks around camp getting everyone assembled just like Christine asked. Once they are all there standing around staring at one another in confusion, Christine says, "First of all, I want to thank you, ST, for finding and saving the life of the man I love. He is here because of you, and I'm here because of him. As soon as Hooty lights this beautiful pile of wood he and DBoR assembled for our enjoyment, I want you to throw everything you own, except the clothes off your backs, into the fire."

FAM is the first to burst out in opposition, "Are you crazy, bitch?

I'm not doing anything of the sort, and neither should any of you."

"Yeah, why should we do anything of the sort? Why should we trust someone we just met?" DBoR shouts.

"Hey, everyone, give the young lady a chance to explain. I'm sure she has good reason for her motives. Isn't that right, Christine?" ST jumps in.

"Being Chief Financial Officer for ROJ's account and for the river rats, I have purchased brand-new six-person tents for everyone, sleeping bags with cots and foam insulation, all new clothes for each and everyone of you, and, yes, you too, FAM. I also have new lounge chairs that won't come apart, hats, and a slew of other personal clothing items. For you, FAM, a complete set of cast-iron cooking pots and kitchen supplies. There's also new packing supplies and coolers. If you see anything you still need, give me a list, and I will see it gets done. Oh yeah, before I forget, everyone has a new canoe, life jackets, and oars. So if there aren't any further questions, Hooty, please light the fire. Before you throw away all your former possessions, you can unload the canoes first, if you don't trust me."

"Christine, being the leader of this camp, please allow me to be the first to accept you as an official river rat. Welcome to our humble abode," ST says.

"Thank you, ST. I am very happy to accept your invitation and to enjoy my new life," Christine replies with delight.

Who knows when any of them have ever ripped into Christmas presents before, but they all were fondling over the new tents—all different colors, of course—ripping open boxes and packages that made their way into the bonfire, and throwing everything that up onto the bank. It was total organized chaos watching them all laughing and cackling like little kids again. ST maintains his composure, of course, taking what is left over and knowing that he could lose a limb if he tries to intervene. He and ROJ sort out what is left, but it is all great stuff. They are both proud to get what they find. As soon as the rest take their supply of new stuff up to their tent site, the old tents, sleeping bags, old used clothes, and of course, the very used lawn chairs found their way into the fire. Different colors reached for the sky as the chemicals in the tents and chairs were consumed by the bonfire.

As soon as all the old stuff was consumed by the fire, all the new supplies were assembled. The new tents went up in no time, and the sleeping bags along with the cots and foam sheets were thrown inside. Everything found its place inside the colorful tents, and the lounge chairs were all displayed with pride just outside the tent flaps. There was laughter and giggling going on the entire time. ROJ and Christine assembled their tent along with a double sleeping bag and extrasoft foam sheet. Their two lounge chairs were interlocking. They were the first to carry their lounge chairs over to the bonfire along with some leftover wine from the last river trip. The others eventually joined, and the laughter continued well into the night.

"Before this exceptional night ends, Christine and ROJ, I want to be the first to say thank you for everything and being so thoughtful to a bunch of river rats," FAM says without any profanities.

"Wow," ROJ finally speaks up, "that was the nicest and most generous thing you have said since I have known you. Thank you for that."

"Well, don't get your hopes up, asswipe. It was just short- lived," FAM replies with her usual self.

"It was nice while it lasted," ROJ says. "Yeah, a whole five seconds," Hooty replies.

ROJ smiles toward ST's direction, and he responds with an approving head nod.

CHAPTER THIRTY-TWO

Morning arrives with ROJ and Christine holding each other in vise grips in their new and very comfortable tent. As he opens one eye to see if Christine is awake yet, he finds her looking right back at him. "Hah, caught you," Christine says. "Thought you could wake up before me?"

"Just wanted to watch you sleep. I have never been this close to you before, and I wanted to cherish the moment," ROJ replies, trying to wipe sleep from his eyes.

"I could go back to sleep again."

"No, that's OK. I cherish just holding you."

"Me too. This is truly wonderful. Didn't know much I would enjoy being outdoors, but I do know that I've had my best sleep in a long time. The fresh air, the sounds along the river, and being with you are a dream come true. I hope it will be like this all the time," Christine says between kisses. "There are no schedules or deadlines to meet. It can be like this all the time, if you want,"

ROJ returns her kisses. "It smells like FAM is using her new kitchen supplies. Let's go see what she has cooked up."

As ROJ and Christine roll out of their tent and stumble over to the fire, FAM greets them with, "It's about time you two pieces of shit made it out of your love cocoon."

"I can see nothing has changed," ROJ says delightfully. Hauling their chairs to the fire, they enjoy a delicious breakfast consisting of bacon, eggs cooked in bacon grease, pancakes cooked in bacon grease, and hash brown potatoes cooked in bacon grease. They can at least enjoy biscuits cooked in the Dutch oven with cooking oil.

"Does she cook everything in bacon grease?" Christine whispers to ROJ.

"No, missy. Just had a lot of bacon that needed to be cooked," FAM replies.

"Well, it does taste great, as long as you love bacon. I guess I'll have to curb my diet to accommodate bacon a lot more," Christine says.

As they try to enjoy their bacon breakfast, ST approaches ROJ. "I was informed of a family who wants to float the thirty-four miles of the Colorado from Redford to here. It's a young couple with a twelve-year- old daughter. What do you think about taking Christine with you to break her in and see how she communicates with the family? If she truly wants to be the Public Relations Officer for the river rats, this will give her great experience," ST explains.

"Sounds great, ST. We need to start somewhere. Why not now?" ROJ says.

"Hey, Christine," ST shouts from across camp. "If you want to be a river rat, you have to have an official name. What's your full name?" ST asks.

"It's Christine Aspen Torrenson. Why?"

"Let's see," ST says. "C-A-T. Oh yeah, CAT. Your river rat name is CAT."

"CAT. Wow. That sounds great. Thanks."

"Well, ROJ, what are you waiting for? We have customers waiting. Let's go," CAT demands.

"I think there's a monster hiding inside you, Christine, I mean,

CAT," ROJ says.

"Just wait till I get started," CAT snaps back. "That's what I'm afraid of," ROJ replies.

"Before coming to the Rio Grande River, I studied it a little so I would know my way around some. Even though I don't know where your accident happened on the river, won't you be canoeing past that area on your guided trips?"

"Yes, that's true."

"How is that going to affect you?"

"I have decided to make it into a positive thing. When I do go through that area, I will respect and admire them for being my parents, and ask GOD to help give me the strength to overcome my emotions and show my tribute to them each time."

"Help me get supplies ready for a one-and-a-half-day canoe trip through the Colorado to Lajitas. We need supplies for lunch and supper," ROJ says.

As they prepare their canoes for the needed supplies including their tent and double sleeping bag, CAT is reminded what she would be doing right now in a different world.

"ROJ, do you realize what I would be doing right now back home?" "That world is gone to me, CAT. You'll have to explain it to me," ROJ answers.

"Right now, I'd be attending the University of Illinois, studying who knows what and partying till who knows what time, wasting away my life and thinking I would actually be accomplishing something. Now that I think about it from a different point of view, I am truly enjoying my life more right now and accomplishing more than I could have ever thought. Of course, my parents would have a different perspective completely, but I really don't give a damn. I'm doing exactly what I want because you are here," CAT says rejoicingly and giving ROJ a kiss.

"Since the accident, I would always choose the life of a river rat. That is what I have become. But, because you found me, and we have become inseparable, you have brought meaning into the life I have chosen. I am so grateful for your sacrifice and consolidating my father's worth. We now have the means to continue doing what we truly love to do. You are the most important person in my life, and always will be. I love you for that," ROJ says in a soft voice CAT has not heard in a very long time.

"You don't know how long I have waited for you to say that, ROJ. I am alive because of who you have become. Your life is my life. I want you to know that. I always want to be with you. I hope you can comprehend that," CAT says.

"I am the one who is blessed because you found me and have brought meaning into my life. You are the reason why I remained strong, waiting for you to find me, and you did. You never gave up on me. You make me strong. Never underestimate your importance in my life. You make me strong," ROJ says firmly.

"I'm glad to know that we complete each other. What do you say we get started and give this young family the time of their lives?" CAT says with utmost confidence.

"You're on, girlfriend." With that, they complete loading their canoes for a leisurely two-day river trip through the Colorado Canyon. They paddle downstream to town where their fare is waiting for them. ROJ gets out of the canoe wading through shallow water to where a young couple is waiting with a cute twelve year old girl wearing a ball cap. Upon seeing the weary daughter, CAT jumps out immediately and focuses her attention on the young girl. She crouches down to her eye level and says, "Hello, my name is CAT, and I'm a river rat who will assist in giving you and your parents the time of your lives on the Rio Grande. Would you like to know what a river rat does?"

"You bet!" the young girl says without hesitation. "What is your name, Sweetie?" CAT asks. "Ronnie."

"I mean your whole name."

"Why do you need my whole name?" Ronnie asks timidly. "In order to be an official river rat, like me, I have to know your whole name so I give you a proper river rat name.""OK. Ronnie Aspen Tomlinson."

"Hey, we both have the same middle name! All right then.

Your river rat name is R-A-T. RAT," CAT says. "I like that! Hey, Mommy, my name is RAT." "That's nice, sweetie," Mrs. Tomlinson says.

They both roll their eyes, and CAT continues educating RAT on what it takes to load a canoe and getting the life jackets to size. RAT follows CAT like a shadow, and they both love the new experience. Meanwhile, ROJ is going over the paperwork and unpleasantries. "I think we have all the paperwork completed. What do you say we get started?" ROJ says.

"Sounds good to me," Mr. Tomlinson says.

"While I back up the trailer to load the canoes for the short ride to Redford where your journey begins, I'll show you how to unpack your suitcases and repack them in the watertight bags.

"RAT, I have a special job for you if you think you are up to it," CAT says.

"Of course, I am. What is it?" RAT replies.

"After these watertight bags are loaded, I need someone like you to blow through this inflator tube to add buoyancy to the bags. Then, I'll show you how to tie them securely in the canoe. How's that sound?"

"Big breaths until the bags are full of air."

After reaching Redford and unloading the canoes on the beach, ROJ parks the shuttle in the parking lot.

"OK, RAT, tie the watertight bags in the canoes like this," CAT shows her.

"OK, Captain ROJ, we are secure and ready to go," CAT says. "Natasha and Frank, where do you want RAT to sit, in your canoe or mine?" ROJ asks.

"I think she'll be much safer in yours. We'll have ourselves to worry about, and that will be enough," Natasha replies.

They push off a little way from shore, and ROJ goes over the different paddle strokes and how to maneuver the canoes. "Natasha and Frank, we will be paddling through mostly calm water, but the Colorado has more rapids than any other canyon on the Rio Grande. Please don't fret. They are very small and very enjoyable. I think RAT will get a real thrill from them."

"We are looking to you to tell us what to do, ROJ, since we have never paddled a canoe before," Frank says.

"No problem. Just shout if you have any questions." After paddling for a mile or so, Natasha belts out, "ROJ, what is that roaring sound?"

"That's just the sound of your first rapid. They will all announce themselves like that," ROJ says.

"Will they get any louder than that?"

"Not likely. All of the rapids are pretty much the same size. After a while, you'll think nothing of it," ROJ tries to calm her fears.

"OK. I sure hope you are right."

RAT seems to be having the most fun, shouting out everything she sees. Her parents seem to be more relaxed after successfully running the first rapid. "Hey, that wasn't so bad!" Natasha shouts.

"I agree, honey. I'm looking forward to more. When is the next rapids, ROJ?" Frank asks.

"I don't know what I'd do if you two were any more excited. I think RAT makes up for all of us. The next set is twenty minutes away. You'll hear it before you see it. Just follow me through the notch like before," ROJ yells.

Both ROJ and CAT are thrilled to see the Tomlinson family relaxed and having the time of their lives, especially RAT. She appears to be fearless. After the third rapids, ROJ shouts over to them, "The tinaja is just ahead. You can get out and walk around or go swimming in a spring fed pool. When we get close, follow me to the beach. I'll get lunch ready!"

"I'm going to do whatever CAT does," RAT says. "Sweetie, I think you need to stay with your parents while I help ROJ get lunch ready," CAT says.

"Since you are officially the public relations officer of the river rats, you should do whatever our customers want to do." "Sounds great. Did you hear that, RAT? What do you want to do?" CAT asks. "I want to go swimming."

They both strip down to their swimming suits worn under their clothes and run to the tinaja. ROJ takes a glance over toward CAT and realizes how beautiful she truly is, especially wearing a swimsuit. The curves of her figure are accentuated in her two-piece swimsuit, and her muscular legs are evident with every step. Natasha and Frank stretch their legs, walking around the beach area. They know their daughter is safe with CAT.

Fifteen minutes later, ROJ announces lunch is ready. He has prepared deli sandwiches, cheeses and veggies with two different dips, and chips, and of course, gorp. As they sit around in a circle, Natasha speaks up, "ROJ and CAT, I can't tell you how easy it is for me to feel completely relaxed being close to nature and seeing our daughter, RAT, totally enjoying herself. She's a tomboy, if you haven't noticed already, but she is so giddy and full of spunk, I don't ever remember her asking so many questions."

"I second that. It was such an odd feeling being so close to the water in these canoes, but it is truly an exhilarating experience. I wish our trip were longer," Frank replies.

"Just think what you have to look forward to when you come back again," ROJ says.

"Well said. What's next, ROJ?" Franks asks.

"There are several more rapids before we camp for the night. The sun goes down rather quickly in these canyon walls, so we'll beach with enough light left to do some more hiking while I prepare supper."

"What is for supper?" Natasha asks.

"It's a surprise, and I have something special for RAT here. By the way, do either of you enjoy a little wine?"

"A special surprise for me? Can't wait!" RAT says. "Yes, ROJ, we enjoy wine," Frank replies.

After packing up lunch, they shove off again. After several rapids later, ROJ points to a beach area with daylight starting to dwindle. They follow him to the beach, secure their canoes, and unpack everything. "CAT will show you how to pitch your tent and assemble everything inside while I start a fire for supper. RAT, what do you want to do?"

"I want to do everything. Where should I begin?"

"Wow, you have more energy than all of us put together!" ROJ exclaims.

"Welcome to our world, ROJ," Natasha says.

"OK, RAT, you can help me untie the bags from the canoe, sort the tent from the watertight bags, then help CAT pitch the tents. If you are still looking for something to do after that, you can help me cook supper. How is that plan?" ROJ says.

"Groovy. Let's get started."

With helper in hand, ROJ unloads the canoe in record time. RAT follows CAT's instructions exceptionally well, pitching the tents. Before ROJ knows it, she right beside him, wanting to help make supper. "I have the fire going. Please unload the chest coolers, and I'll let you know what I need first. By the way, don't unwrap the foil thing. That's your surprise."

RAT's eyes get big as pie plates, and a huge smile fills her face. All the while she's unloading the coolers, her eyes gravitate toward the foil thing, just like a kid's in a candy store.

"Natasha and Frank, how do you like your steaks cooked?" ROJ yells across the beach.

"Oh my gosh. That is your surprise?" Natasha asks. "Just part of it. So how do you like your's cooked?" ROJ asks again.

"Both medium, and medium well for RAT," she says. "Come on over and make yourselves comfortable. RAT, please open all those containers and put spoons in them, please," ROJ says.

As ROJ assembles their supper into an organized fashion, Natasha and Frank are mesmerized to see all the wonderful things ROJ put together for supper. Along with marinated top sirloin steaks, he is also cooking huge Idaho potatoes, green beans, corn, and cranberries, and setting out huge amounts of butter as well as chocolate chip cookies. There are also leftover chips with cheese as well as veggies for munchies. They can't further believe what is happening when he pulls out a gallon of white wine and begins to pour each one of them a glass.

"ROJ, I had no idea we would be eating a gourmet meal on the Rio Grande in the middle of nowhere. You are truly awesome, and this is an exceptional experience I could not have possibly imagined," Frank says in total delight.

"The river rats aim to please—CAT and me—that is. It is our pleasure to make this journey worth remembering with the hopes you will return to extend your journey with us," ROJ answers.

"Well, if this is any indication of what we can expect in longer river trips with you, we are definitely sold."

"Thank you very much for your vote of confidence. Your steaks are ready to take off, and the potatoes are also ready. Just relax and enjoy your meal. Don't be bashful to ask for seconds or more wine, this is all for your family," ROJ says.

The total look of delight and satisfaction on the faces of the Tomlinson family makes CAT realize she made the right decision to stay with ROJ. He has truly grown and embraced his life as a river rat, and it shows in his actions and how he lights up when engaging with his customers. She can't see him—or herself—doing anything else.

"I can't eat another bite. You have really outdone yourself, ROJ," Frank says.

"Hey, what about my surprise, ROJ?" RAT demands.

"I could never forget you, RAT. You can open that foil thing now."

She very carefully opens it, and to delight that fills her face, she takes out a huge slice of carrot cake full of icing and starts stuffing it in her mouth.

"How did you know that was her favorite?" Natasha asks. "Just a lucky guess, but I can tell she is really enjoying herself with as much cake on her face as in her mouth," ROJ replies.

"I think with a short walk along the beach, I'll be ready for bed. Coming, honey?" Natasha says. "You too, RAT."

While the Tomlinson family takes a stroll along the beach, all hand in hand, CAT gives ROJ a huge smile of approval as they clean up from supper. Getting everything packed up for breakfast, which will come quick enough, CAT finally says, "ROJ, darling, I know now why you chose this type of life. It feels right for me too. I want you to know that."

"I can't tell you how long I have been waiting for you to say those words. I am the one who feels truly honored to be together with you. You are the one who came looking for me, and I'd do anything to keep us together for now on," ROJ says, giving her a huge hug. As CAT begins crying, they walk hand in hand to their tent and fall asleep in each other's arms. The next morning arrives with coffee on the boil while CAT is still sleeping. Smelling the coffee, CAT replies, "ROJ, why didn't you wake me? I wanted to help you get everything ready. Remember, we do things together."

"Being public relations officer has its perks. It means you don't have to get up early to start breakfast," ROJ says jokingly. "I'll have to look at my job description and maybe make a slight amendment."

"You do that, until then, I am the boss, and you can get up whenever you're ready."

Frank is next to roll out of bed, followed by RAT. "What time is it?"

Natasha asks sticking her head out of the tent.

"Left my watch in the car. Sorry, can't help you. I know it's time to eat breakfast," Frank says.

While Frank makes his way toward the fire, he stops in midstride. "ROJ, what have you made us for breakfast? It looks like a feast."

"Well, it probably is. Especially if you're hungry. Come on and pull up a log to sit on."

"I thought supper was a feast not to be surpassed, but this spread you have put out for us looks outstanding. Honey, come here and look what ROJ has prepared for us!" Frank shouts with delight.

"ROJ, what have you done now to get my husband's feathers so ruffled?"

Natasha makes her way to the fire, and she too stops in her stride when she sees what ROJ has prepared. All around the grill, on top of red- hot smoldering coals, sits a huge pot of coffee, a skillet full of scrambled eggs with butter, toast on the side with jam and honey available, hash brown potatoes, bacon and sausage, leftover cookies, orange and apple juice. "If I go back home gaining weight, I am going to blame you, ROJ," Natasha jokingly says.

"That's the point. Want to make sure you don't leave hungry." "No chance of that," Frank says.

"When you all finish breakfast, CAT will show you how to fold up your tent and get your belongings stuffed back into the watertight bags. I'll have breakfast packed up as well by then," ROJ says.

As Natasha and Frank take their tent and bag to the canoe, RAT asks her mother, "Can I be a river rat like CAT when I grow up, Mommy? I have learned so much from her already."

"We'll see, sweetheart. We'll see." Seeing the semi- disappointment on RAT's face, she gives in and says, "OK, show me what you have learned."

RAT immediately dives in and says, "In order to securely pack everything in the canoe, you must start by...

The End